3 ⁹⁵

Over The Hill

Reflections on Ageism Between Women

By Baba Copper

THE CROSSING PRESS / FREEDOM, CALIFORNIA 95019

Acknowledgments

The words on page 1 appeared in the essay by Baba Copper, "Notes from the Fifty-ninth Year," in *Sinister Winsdom*, no. 10 Summer 1979.

"The View from Over the Hill" first appeared, in an earlier version, in *Trivia*, no. 7, Summer 1985.

"Old, not Other" first appeared in *The Women's Review of Books*, April 1986.

"Growing Old in the Mainstream" first appeared in *Off Our Backs*, vol. xiv, no. 10, Nov. 1984.

"A Different Kind of Love Quarrel" first appeared in *Common Lives/Lesbian Lives*, no. 17, Fall 1985.

"Voices: On Becoming Old Women" first appeared in *Women and Aging, An Anthology*, a special issue of *Calyx*, vol. 9, no. 2 & 3, Winter 1986.

Cover design by Betsy Bayley

Cover photo by Pia Chamberlain

Printed in the U.S.A.

Library of Congress Cataloging-in-Publication Data

Copper, Baba.
  Over the hill.

  1. Aged women — Psychology. 2. Aged women — Public opinion. I. Title. II. Title: Ageism between women.
HQ1061.C654   1988   305.4   88-1189
ISBN 0-89594-308-5
ISBN 0-89594-302-6 (pbk.)

Patriarchal reversal teaches us to do things against our own best interests — rationalizing them, psychologizing them, minimizing them — while at the same time taking the blame for them upon ourselves and socializing our daughters to do the same. We are taught to expect certain things when we get older — all negative — all diminishing. The only way that women who are young now can evade that fate is by seeing to it that it doesn't happen to me.

Foreword

A decade has passed in which I have written and talked about the collision of ageism with my positive exploration of the years past sixty. These essays and excerpts from my journals represent my endeavor to analyze and resist the false assumptions about aging ingrained in my own psyche and in the society as a whole which diminished my pursuit of happiness. The experience of growing old varies greatly in women, depending upon such factors as class or economic resources (often without overlap), racial or religious or ethnic traditions of our communities, and our health. My perspective as an old lesbian may seem very remote to some of my readers. However, all old women, regardless of their differences, share a common burden: the prejudice and stereotyping ageism brings.

Ageism, not aging, oppresses us. We are oppressed by other women and we oppress ourselves. Although many of the details in this book are drawn from my life, *they are not the story of my aging*, which has yet to be told. Rather, this is a collection of reflections about a social malaise under which all old women suffer, even though they may not even be aware of their suffering, even though they do not have the words to describe it.

There has been a conspiracy of silence about ageism both in the women's movement and among those professionals who provide services for the old. A multi-billion dollar industry focuses on the special needs of people over sixty who are perceived as retired, government-subsidized consumers of age-specific products and services. In the two hundred subheadings for possible presentations to the 34th Annual meeting of the American Society on Aging in 1988, ranging from Contracts and Grant Management to Suicide, the word ageism never appeared. Nor is one likely to hear it at any conference on age, even from the old gerontologists.

As I say repeatedly in the pieces in this book, ageism

exists because it rearranges power relations between people. Those who "service the elderly" are trained not to identify with them, but to make decisions for them, to "expedite" filling their needs. Old people, like most involuntary consumers, are easier to manage if they see themselves as powerless.

Even more serious than the professionals' blindness to their own ageism has been the slowness of feminists to recognize the theoretical and experiential importance of female-focused ageism, not just in its impact on old women but for all women. As feminist theory gradually has revealed the extent of women's internalization of oppression, women have changed the patriarchy by changing who we are, who we expect ourselves to be. Yet this work has only begun on the terrible cancer of the fear and loathing of old age which saps so much of all women's energy.

It is for these reasons that I have written about my own experience of ageism between women. As long as we are busy dreading each year beyond thirty, trying desperately to convince ourselves and others that the accumulation of years has not really changed us — that we are still one of the girls — none of us will have the wit or the energy to benefit from the gains we have made in the sixties, the seventies, the eighties.

Most would agree that ageism is *not* the total experience of age for women. But only if we learn to recognize ageism — name it, resist it, refine our understanding of it, stop participating in it — only then can we separate growing old from the fog of ageism which diminishes us. Then, and only then, are true acceptance and celebration of age possible.

Inventing My Life

I am a woman who has chosen to live out the last third — maybe even more — of my life in a state of voluntary marginality, embracing an identity named deviant by society. The dictionary meaning of the word "deviant" is to turn aside from an appointed way, with actions and beliefs which differ from the expectations of the culture. At fifty-one I turned aside from the traditional roles of wife and mother. I came out as a lesbian. This was and is a path of choice for me, a needed escape.

I walked away from the ground which women usually try to hold onto — security of family and status — recompense for the nurturance and labor we provide with our lives. I did this after a full exploration of female "normalcy" which I found deficient on all counts, a wasteland. I yearned for deviance.

As I burned my bridges behind me I believed that in my own way I was a pioneer like my foremothers. I was inventing my life as well as reflecting the movement of women in the 1960s. I knew nothing of the repeated her-story, the waves of ingenuity women have shown to develop life styles which evaded male exploitation. Feminist scholarship had not yet unveiled the communities of women such as the Beguines, or the lively, independent nuns of the walled cities within cities of the Visroyalty of Peru. Patriarchal erasure had successfully withheld from me the choices that other women had made before me which might have provided models for my own rebellion. Even the strong women of my own line who had not married or when widowed refused new alliances I looked at as rejects.

At the time of my flight from normalcy, I did not recognize that other state of marginality I was entering, the stigma accorded to age in women. Being middle aged, I had only a rudimentary feeling for the deviance of female aging. I knew only that there was a world I could join where women were generating ideas which shredded my unexamined suppositions. That world encouraged me to confront the perspectives and ways of being which I had never found comfortable and which could no longer hold me. I failed to notice that the women in that community were young women.

Since the time when I came out, lesbianism has lost some of its force as deviance, especially for lesbians. Radical lesbian feminism has been a powerful tool in debunking the demands of patriarchy for heterosexual normalcy. More and more young women know of the choice that was hidden from me and move into the world of women without suffering any stigmatized self-conception, despite the continuing homophobia of the society at large. But the stigma of age has not been subjected to the same siege of ideas and consciousness raising, in the larger world or among lesbians.

My age makes many of my social situations among lesbians uneasy. There is a gap between the needs of my personality and the tactful distance women put between me and them. *I* am the one who is expected to relieve this social tension, *I* am the one who must gain greater acceptance by breaking through their prejudices. Sometimes I wonder what growing old would have been like for me had I not rushed toward being an outsider. There are horrors which I know I have escaped: the guilt and disparagement old women suffer as the old men in their lives lose sexual potency; the terrible insecurity fostered by competition with younger women for men; the humiliation and self-sacrifice built into the role of grandmother.

But perhaps my relationships with my female peers would have been easier had I not become a lesbian. Lesbians are women who do not deny the component of eroticism which flows between all human beings. At the same time, their traditional female socialization to age-passing and incest-taboo (eroticism toward the mother figure) is firmly in place, as unchallenged as that of any heterosexual woman. Despite lesbian rebellion against heterosexual normalcy, we are poor at finding ways to bond with old women without the familiar, familial safety nets.

On Being a Rebellious Old Woman

I live in Vacation Land. Come summer, Main Street is bumper to bumper with RV's filled with aging tourists. True, the lines of foam breaking the indigo of the sea against the pine tufted cliffs attract all ages of city folk, searching for places where Nature is still winning over tourism. But a lot of the people here aren't vacationers; they are retirees, old people like me, come to live full time in their vacation homes. Lots of old men, with their middle-aged wives in tow. Sport fishermen, pulling boats behind their Winnebagos, burdened with all their equipment. The local Safeway has lots of wide spaces in the parking lot marked "RV ONLY." I go to Safeway more to study my contemporaries than to benefit from the dubious specials. In the long lines of the computer-equipped checkout stands, I can stare with impunity at the living norms of my generation — norms untouched by poverty or racial differences — Americans who have made it into the golden years.

Why am I so curious about a group I should know as well as anyone, being one of them? I am not poor; I live in a lovely little house near the sea, crafted by me to fit exactly the needs of my later years. I am white and able-bodied. But I don't fit the norm. Months, sometimes even years, go by without my seeing a woman I can identify with — one who signals resistance to the role fulfillment expected of my age/sex bracket. Nor do I find them in TV or advertisements or the movies. Even more disturbing is the absence of my image in books. Until the strong, honest face of Barbara Macdonald accosted me from the cover of *Look Me in the Eye*,[1] and I found words inside that book which matched some of my experience, it was possible to view myself as one of a kind, unique.

What is so strange about me? I am a woman like hundreds of others I know who is trying to tinker with my life choices — to fit them as best I can to what I have learned from feminist analysis. I am simply a woman saying *no* to some patriarchal expectations and conditioning. I say *no* to the extent that I am able to refuse without threatening my basic survival. Unfortunately, other women like me are young, whereas I am old. The rebellious young share signals of their mutiny with other women of their own age. They have not thought about the possibility of a rebellious old woman. In fact, to the extent that older women are part of their support system, their stability, the base they can exploit as they wrestle their due from the Fathers, they are not really ready for me. I become an exception.

If there is any position I fear, it is that of the exceptional woman. In my pre-liberation days, I hid a lot from myself by believing that I was an exception—exceptionally gifted and exceptionally difficult. I was flattered when someone told me I thought like a man. Now I would be insulted. But again, as I have grown older and more radical, it becomes convenient to slip into personalizing the politics of my situation.

For instance, I am a grandmother. My struggles to make my married daughters understand that I must relate to this role differently—or not at all—have failed miserably. No one is interested in my need for negotiation.

How do we change? Am I alone in questioning the assumptions about my time, my affections, my willingness to buy or bribe allegiance, the availability of my services and space? I have raised four children; my mothering instincts are worn exceedingly thin. Why is it up to me to bear the brunt of refusal, withdrawal? With so many grandmothers in the world, am I the only one who wants things to be different?

Recently I read about the revolutionary heroine of Nicaragua's Foreign Ministry, a lawyer and single mother of five. In the view of the writer as well as the revolutionary herself, she is a feminist. Since a busy career leaves her little time for her children, "her widowed mother takes care of them." It is much the same in the Soviet Union and China, where revolution has opened up opportunities for younger women, taking them out of the home while grandmothers are expected to pick up the slack. In China the grandmothers now will have only one grandchild to raise because of the decrees of the Fathers, while in Nicaragua and the Soviet Union, the State controls female reproduction in the other direction, by withholding abortion and contraceptive information. This is socialist feminist progress?

First the men unload responsibility for their children upon women, then women become liberated and unload their children on their old mothers. It is quite irrelevant that there are ethnic, religious and class taboos against anything but joyful acceptance of these expectations in the old women themselves. Liberation for women means old women too. I know that these grandmothers are often the ones who insist that they want to do what they are doing, who resist the attempts of governments to limit births, who insist that grandchildren give them a reason for living. I also recognize that the old women in the United States often unwillingly live far away from their grandchildren. None of this legitimizes exploiting old women in unpaid jobs which repeat the stresses of their child rearing years. Service is not necessarily the *function* of age in women.

When I came out at fifty-one, it was my hope to escape from the pernicious roles and expectations of heterosexuality into a world where my goal would be personal growth. I wanted my personal choices to be politicized by the question "Who profits and who loses from this?" I wanted to fashion my relationships so that neither I nor another would be used — that elusive utopia of equality within intimacy. Although I am not adverse to nurturing others, I want my last years to reflect personal potentials which were suppressed in me as a young and mid-life woman. It is important to me that I do not submerge my identity in any female service role, least of all with my grandchildren.

The Grandmother Blues

I understand the resistance of lesbian literary magazines to the idea of a "specialist monitor" who would scan for the politically offensive — the ageist or ableist content that so often slips by the young and the able. But there is reason to be alarmed by the ageist content or lack of content I see constantly in the print media.

For instance, there is the grandmother as portrayed in poems and stories by younger women. I have no clear formula to solve this problem. I am not even sure how many old women find it tiresome. I know that I am terribly jumpy whenever I read the word "grandmother"— but that does not mean that all the memories of grandmothers are ageist. I certainly do not want grandmothers to become a forbidden subject.

A long time ago I worked with a collective on a mothers/daughters issue of a feminist magazine. I was the only mother of adult daughters in the group; most were either simply daughters or mothers of babies or little girls. I announced at the first meeting that, among other things, I was there to see to it that there would be no mother-trashing in the issue. The women were horrified. They raised the bogyman of *Censorship*. I tried to illuminate the different ways of dealing with our anger at our mothers without blaming them for everything. However, most of the women in the group believed that mothers deserved what they got and found my continuing resistance deeply frustrating.

We aren't usually angry at grandmothers so we seldom trash them. Like mothers they serve us. We may feel superior to them because they were less educated or were old fashioned (we like that, as well); often we were taught not to take them seriously. So now when they are safely out of our lives, we use the memory of them to evoke nostalgia — less assimilated ethnicity, less complicated times, the security of ascribed relationships.

At the same time, what we grandmothers are doing

with our lives, the problems we face *now*, the present true state of our relationships, the issues which we might raise as important — *our priorities* — are not considered interesting. These are never the subject of poems or political analysis by younger women. If they *do* break this rule, they are often punished by a rebuff from publishers who believe that "old ladies don't sell." The expectation that old women are focused in an obsolete past is so strong that even women writers who have aged sitting at their typewriters seldom write about the experience of their later years. A notable exception to this is May Sarton with her *At Seventy*[2] and *As We Are Now*.[3] Most old women writers do not want to say, "This is what I am thinking now that I am old, and it differs from what I used to think in thus and such way" because they correctly fear that no one will read it. Even a writer of the stature of Doris Lessing felt impelled to publish her novel about old age, *The Diaries of Jane Somers*,[4] under a false name. So, with very few exceptions, our writing remains age-closeted. We pretend to ourselves that nothing has changed but our bodies, that our perceptions are just the same as middle-aged women. The unique insights of our time of life are erased by age assimilation.

We feminists are guilty of refusing to resist this male esthetic. When we old women try to raise the consciousness of feminists to ageism, we are asking politicized women to clean up their act, to rethink our relationship to our most intimate oppressors — the ones against whom we have rebelled — our mothers. It is not surprising that the issue is so loaded.

Mother-Blaming

When Freud discovered that the primary source of all personal problems was the mistaken socialization we received at the hands of our mothers, the Otherness of old women received its most potent scholarly justification. Not only did he instill disabling guilt and tension in every middle-aged mother, but he also placed a terrible weapon of mistrust and scapegoating in the hands of women, to be used against the women whom they see as the Other, the older, the one with whom they do not compete.

Growing up in the patriarchy is almost guaranteed to create neurosis in a woman. If we can just be kept focused (with the help of our well paid therapist) on the sins of the mother, we will never need to take responsibility for our own shit. Certainly we will find no reason to revolt against men. We are encouraged to believe that our pain is the fault of the (m)Other, who deserves what she gets from us.

More Mother-Blaming

I remember when I had three babies and was losing my mind. All three sick at once. No sleep. Nothing for me, ever. I'm not sure that I fully understood how fragile my hold on sanity was, but I do remember feeling totally abandoned by my mother. I would sit at my sewing machine making clothing for the kids, singing *Sometimes I Feel Like a Motherless Child*, feeling terrible nostalgia for my shipfitter days when I wore a hard hat and earned time-and-a-half on Saturdays. Those were the late 1940s, before we women had figured out that we were programmed to fulfill somebody else's goals. In the grip of patriotic economic myths, we really believed that we had chosen our own destiny.

As a mother I knew I was miserable. But the only one who was hard to forgive was my mother. All through my childhood she had given me a hard sell of wife-and-motherhood, despite the fact that she was a professional and a single mother, earning her keep and mine. I considered myself much too modern, too sophisticated to be influenced by my mother. Nevertheless, I now realize that I bought the values she advocated. It was she whom I resented, whom I felt abandoned by, even though my independence from her had been one of my primary motivations in getting married in the first place. Never mind that I was thirty years old. Never mind that she was in her sixties, a single woman supporting herself in another city.

I am much older and much wiser now. I move among lesbians younger than myself. Now I am the surrogate for their resentments against their mothers. I am a walking reminder that they will someday lose the delicious irresponsibility which is the power of their youth.

The View from Over the Hill

Youth sees itself as immune to the threat of aging. I can remember the day when I used the phrase "over the hill" to describe an old woman. The implications of the phrase and my complicity in those implications never crossed my mind. Now from experience I understand that someone over the hill is metaphorically out of sight. In my youthful complacency, by using that phrase I was banishing old age from my awareness. Now that I am old, I have become increasingly curious about why I needed to reassure myself in this way.

Every woman gets older from the day she is born, but there are great variations in the impact of this fact upon different lives and upon different times in those lives. There are endless unexamined contradictions in the prejudice which women feel toward the old women they themselves are or are becoming. Lesbian ageism is probably the ultimate extension of these self-defeating contradictions. It is this that I need to examine, since the greater part of my experience of ageism has been with lesbians. As the years beyond fifty-eight have accumulated, I have found it increasingly difficult to participate in the social and political life of the lesbian community. This difficulty has reflected a change in my status as ascribed by other women, not in my capacity for effective or enjoyable involvement. A subtle transition has taken place in which I have slipped from the category of "tolerated" (passing for middle aged) to a new and shunned identity which has no name but "old."

The old woman finds herself captured by stereotypes which drain her initiative and shatter her self-respect. The mythical prototypes of the Wicked Old Witch with unnatural powers, the Old Bad Mother with neurotic power needs, and the Little Old Lady, ludicrously powerless, cloud the individuality of every woman past sixty. Since childhood all of us have been bombarded by systematic distortions of female aging in fairy tales, legends, books, movies, plays and

TV. Age prejudice encourages substitution of these manufactured realities for the real human being with real personal powers whom we encounter. Ageism rationalizes the discarding of old women — as workers, friends, lovers, relatives.

Feminism has taught me to scrutinize closely male reversals of women's truths. The blatant reversal of old women's reality, not only in our culture, but cross-culturally and down through patriarchal history, tells me something about the psychological and political needs which stereotypes such as the Wicked Old Witch fulfill. *One of the primary definitions of patriarchy is the absence of old women of power.* Simmering in the psyche of the Father are his ancient fears of the old matriarch and her potential use of power; preferential treatment of her daughters over her sons; matrilineal inheritance; incitement to resistance against the institution of marriage; or support for the insubordination of a daughter to a husband. The accumulated experience of old women has always been a part of what Adrienne Rich called "the enormous potential counterforce (to patriarchy) that is having to be restrained."[5]

I believe that there is an important reservoir of lesbian energy denied by this false consciousness, this "othering" of the old lesbian. Access to that reservoir of energy is guarded by women acting upon unexamined traditions, attitudes rooted in the commonplace. They are rewarded by increased power within our limited world. But in carrying the double-edged sword of ageism, they wound themselves. Ultimately, they serve the interests of male dominance.

One of the pledges I made when I found myself going "over the hill" was that I would learn to articulate the great complexity of the experience of ageism as it takes place between women. Detailing the particulars, especially the startling erosion of the relative safety of middle age, will not satisfy me. Rather, I need to explore the root sources of my dilemma, speculating about the conscious and unconscious motivations of the women who seek to diminish me. I recognize that my present and future pain is identical to that which I have caused others. It is time that we stop this inter-generational warfare. I would like to believe that I am not the only one dissatisfied with the low priority which lesbian feminism has assigned to these divisions between us.

Inventing Lesbian Identity — Who We Are, or Could Be

If lesbianism ever becomes a mass phenomenon, it will be because it offers women the opportunity to explore a fundamentally new social identity. No longer subject to male sexual choice, we learn not only to choose, but to decide for ourselves on what ethical and erotic basis to make choices of all kinds. Without being particularly conscious of what we are doing, lesbians are collectively forging an unprecedented female identity through the living of our lives.

Choices are often made on the basis of assumptions. The assumptions which we make automatically and unconsciously in default of rational decisions are the vast ground of all human relations. They are as necessary to action as being able to breathe without awareness. But default assumptions are often intimately tied to nuances of hierarchy, which in turn falsely inform our identity or sense of self. It is here that lesbian choices need politically guided attention. Patriarchal standards of taste — rules of esthetic and erotic choices — perpetuate male structures of power. If we allow male defined standards of choice to be our default standards, we maintain female powerlessness. We waste the opportunity which our lesbianism provides: to choose how to choose.

This is particularly true in relation to age prejudice, since so many of the default assumptions which diminish a woman as she ages are derived from sexism. Male contempt for the older woman as unfit for the reproducer/sex object roles filled by younger women (still the primary source of female power in the patriarchy) is the foundation of the old woman's powerless position. Being largely barred from the working world further diminishes our status. If we are not sex objects or breeders or caretakers or wage workers, we are loathsome since it is these *roles* which make females legitimate in male judgment. As Susan Sontag, in her deeply ageist and heterosexist article, "The Double Standard of Aging,"[6] pointed out: "That old women are repulsive is one of the most profound esthetic and erotic feelings in our culture."

Lesbians, the group within women's culture most self-conscious about patriarchal values, cultivate the illusion that we waltz to our own tunes. Yet lesbians, like everyone else, are all getting older. Our community is so ill-prepared for this that old lesbians find themselves disappearing right off the edge of reality. The ageism we encounter teaches us that we are obsolete; that we should not be able to imagine ourselves powerful, either physically or socially. It is a standard default assumption of the lesbian political community that old lesbians are conservative (or at least politically incorrect) and inflexible. Above all else we are expected to be submissive to women younger than ourselves who are the "right" age to exert power within the lesbian world. We are asked to be walking contradictions to the cliches of lesbian identity which all of us are in the process of inventing. Unless old lesbians are re/membered as sexual, attractive, useful, integral parts of the woman-loving world, current lesbian identity is a temporary mirage, not a new social statement of female empowerment.

Why Haven't We Heard More About Ageism Before?

In trying to understand ageism, I find few guides beyond my own feelings and experience. With the notable exception of Barbara Macdonald and Cynthia Rich's book, *Look me in the Eye*,[7] there has been no real analysis of ageism from the feminist community. Susan Sontag did not question the cultural rejection of old women. Instead, she pleaded for a time extension of the acceptance which passing provides for the middle years. Her primary contribution in "The Double Standard of Aging" was to distinguish between the male and female experiences of aging.

Even the more subtle discrimination suffered by mid-life women has rarely been examined. Attention has focused instead on the "real" problems, those named by women in their twenties and thirties. It is as if ageism were a minor difficulty, something which can be cured easily by a little "right" thinking. Since few differentiate between the adultism which young people suffer as they grow up, the ageism men experience, and the primal loathing and stereotyping which hit women when they grow old, people assume they know what ageism is and how it feels. Sometimes it is included in the litany of "isms" with which we exhort each other, sometimes not.

My breaking the silence which surrounds ageism feels very unsafe to me. By demanding that younger women share with old women the respect and power generated among women, I am questioning younger women's use of that power. (The hill I am descending is a hill of power.) More than this, I would like to destroy their smug closet of "age-refuge"—those safe, dishonest, inner denials of the process of aging. All women practice age passing as a method of coping with whatever aging "crisis" we currently imagine threatens our self-esteem, from sixteen to ninety. Age passing, like any other kind of passing, involves lying first to others and ultimately to one's self. By raising the issues of passing and power and identity, I am engaging in activities which are forbidden to my kind. Old women who find fault are seen as Bad Mothers. They are not forgiven, and they are ostracized.

Why, you may ask, haven't old women raised these issues in the past fifteen years of women's negotiations with each other? I think the answer to this lies in the peculiarities of the experience of aging itself. Unlike other oppressions by class or ethnicity or race, oppression by age steals upon us gradually, invading the defenses carefully constructed against it. Passing begins long before the ritually endowed age of thirty. It begins when women (lesbians included) start equating youth and well-being. Age passing becomes a state of mind, a measure of self-worth, a guide to choice. When we reflect "young" tastes in our clothing, cosmetics, activities, friends and lovers, we are passing. As Sontag pointed out back in 1977, growing older for women is mainly an ordeal of the imagination—the biological eventuality dims in comparison with the social judgment. As ageist negative experience begins to impinge seriously on our self-image, we deny that we are getting older. At the same time, we deepen our reliance upon whatever advantages our relative youth may provide us. The age acceptance which we need from others we refuse ourselves. Women in their forties and fifties, themselves victims of ageism, are often the most vicious in dealing with women older than themselves. Many old women become increasingly ageist and self-hating, decade by decade, from sixty to ninety.

It isn't just ageism that sneaks up on us. The process of growing old—biological aging—involves constant adjustments of one's responses and goals. Old age acts as a thief in the comfortable storeroom of the expected, forcing one to adapt to changes which arrive as strangers to the usual patterns of be-ing developed over the years. It is important that these adaptations, or losses—if that is what they prove to be—are met as courageously as possible. Old women need positive reinforcement from others to meet these strangers.

What we do *not* need is silencing. Yet the single strongest social message an old woman receives is to "grow old gracefully"—*not to burden others* with complaints. By complaining, an elder will only increase her isolation—or so the saying goes. This threat obscures for old women the importance of naming our experience honestly.

Not all of the pain "on the other side of the hill" is inevitable. Much of it is simply serving the interests and increasing the power of others. As long as lesbians see ourselves as empowered by diminishing other lesbians, then old women become good targets for these interactions. Most important, women of all ages must acknowledge that the political quiet surrounding ageism is simply more female compliance in patriarchal values.

Is This What Young Lesbians Really Want?

Conforming to the Little Old Lady stereotype of absolute powerlessness should not be a goal for any lesbian, yet the pressure I feel going "over the hill" is to behave less assertively—to be "appropriately" submissive. This is the subliminal message from women as well as men. It says: "Smile, or you will be seen as critical or grouchy! If you manage to camouflage your white hair or your wrinkles or your limp, then you will be more likely to deserve attention. You will be more acceptable." If you can't pass, then you must act powerless.

I feel as if I am involved in some subtle competition not of my own making. Although feminist lesbians attempt to resist participation in power/over scenarios, we still listen carefully for the subtle indicators of respect from other women. Sources of power such as looks, skills, sexual confidence, resources, political correctness—all play their part in the complex process of figuring out whether one is "ahead" (and feeling confident and easy) or "behind" (and feeling uncomfortable). Although old women often receive deference, I seldom experience a feeling of real respect from others. Almost never do I sense that I am being approached by a younger woman in the spirit of acceptance, learning or wonder.

I am confined within my category—an old woman, potential scapegoat. I do not mean to say that all my experience is negative all the time. But the fear, contempt and rage which many women unconsciously carry for old women are latent. The discharge of these irrational feelings is postponed only to the moment when I do not please. *I feel like a walking lightning rod.*

Over and over, I have had the same experience, both with lesbians near my age and younger. When I exert my powers on "their side," in agreement or in service to them, all is well. The mirror they hold up to me reflects "capable, intuitive, likable, creative, interesting." But when I exert myself in my own interests or defense, I find that I am punished. What they want — no, demand — from me is unconditional love, support and service. Their effort to control my behavior takes many forms, but is often distinguished by explosive intensity or irrational anger. Suddenly I get lots of negativity and trashing, not the "I feel" kind but the accusatory "You are" kind. I have become the Bad Mother or the Wicked Witch. Then their mirror says "self-centered, overpowering, coercive, withholding."

I, in turn, must process this feedback through the filter of my years. Have I suddenly gone through some startling personality change which makes me radically different from the woman I was ten, twenty, thirty years before? What about the lesbian identity I am struggling to perfect — assertive, un-self-sacrificing, honest? How can I gauge whether or not these women are being ageist? Maybe this is the way they always act. But why, then, am I having so many of these experiences in the last few years? Why do other women refuse to negotiate differences with me? What about our feminist determination to work things through, to refuse to treat each other as men have treated us? The self-doubt built into these questions is bottomless. Always I ask myself, "Are you too sensitive? Is this awkwardness perhaps *your* fault?"

I do not have answers. All I can do is list some of the ways in which old lesbians may find ourselves used within the lesbian community. Some are from personal experience, some from watching the experience of other old women. (Obviously not all women participate in these offenses, nor do all old women experience them, nor are they limited to interactions between lesbians.)

The old woman is one whose labor/energy can be assimilated by everyone. We are someone to listen to others' troubles without telling ours. We are the dump where others are free to unload. It is considered politically correct to extract money or favors from us without a fair exchange of goods, labor or services. We are subject to a different code of honor than other women. For instance, an old woman who owns her own home, who is near retirement from a good paying job, or who has a little capital from a divorce settlement, may be branded as a rich woman. The age barrier to further income from wages — a barrier which radically changes old women's relationship to capital — is ignored with youthful chauvinism. We are a Class Enemy. We can be envied with impunity, ripped off with righteous indignation. Any resistance we muster in our own defense is punished severely. *Self-defense is absolutely unallowable in a mother figure*.

There is a look of wary readiness in the eyes of many old women. Our bodies often unconsciously reflect our humiliation. We have demonstrated a remarkable ability to internalize our own coercion. The body language of many old women speaks of our position at the age/sex nadir — the ones no one wants to be. We are seen as the cause of many frustrations, disappointments and failures. The emphasis is laid upon our differences, our faults, our style, our mistakes, the general *difficulty* in dealing with us. Although our experience, perhaps our expertise, is needed, others avoid ceding to us either leadership or credit. In typical patterns of rationalization, almost everyone agrees that we *ourselves* are the ones who caused the offenses committed against us. Once we are found guilty, judgment is passed from mouth to mouth, with everyone else hearing about it but us. Often we are unsure of what the real accusation is. We are usually short of allies, social power, and self-love. It is through interactions like these that women carry out the horizontal violence against ourselves, using our energies to do the essential work of preserving "woman's place."

I try to be the kind of person everyone likes. I listen well, I nurture, I create goodies, and I give comfort. I touch others even though I am seldom touched. I don't complain a lot. I suppress my needs, ignore the contempt or sexual invisibility I experience. (I bite my tongue and walk around as if on eggs!) I find myself metamorphosed into the stereotypical granny, even though I judge the role intolerably demeaning. This violation of Self is unhealthy, as feminists have been quick to testify in relation to male definitions of appropriate heterosexual female behavior or femininity. The personality I feel I am being asked to assume as an old woman is even more docile/submissive than that asked of me as a young woman throughout my life with men. It is the polar opposite of the independent assertive dyke that I smashed my traditional world into bits to become.

Whose Mother Are We Defeating and Why?

There is no way to talk about ageism between women without focusing on mother/daughter relations. Sometimes I feel as if ageism is misnamed; that the problem should be called Daughterism. One of the ways that a young woman can get a taste of her future is to be turned into a mother-figure by a peer, who may or may not be older. At the lesbian summer camp of Califia, where all are invited to generate workshops, I spontaneously wrote *Daughterism* on the schedule, interested to see how other women would respond. Forty young women showed up, eager to describe their confusion over being used as a mother by friends, fellow workers, or lovers. Thematic to their testimony was self-blaming speculation as to why their *looks* evoked this manipulative behavior in others. ("I just know that it is because I have big breasts!") None had any theoretical framework with which to view her misery. From *my* vantage point, at that time nearly over the hill, all these women were potential daughters, capable of using me as they had been used.

I have often wondered if it wouldn't be possible to make a fortune by manufacturing a T-shirt which, in large letters across the breasts, said: I AM NOT YOUR MOTHER. Most older women find themselves stereotyped as mothers by younger women. This erasure of our individuality is unfair, but the psychological underside is downright ugly. If the older woman triggers childhood angst in the younger, the older may find herself bearing a burden of projected hostility without the slightest clue as to what is going on. (Psychologists seem to agree that many people need to recreate unresolved childhood experience.) All women have been taught to see mothers as fair prey, to be used as the giver-who-does-not-get.

The other side of the mother/daughter coin is the legitimate rage of the daughter for being raised by her mother to fulfill goals that are largely in violation of her own self-realization, especially when seen though lesbian eyes. With few exceptions, lesbians have in common the experience of growing up mothered by a woman who abided by traditional patriarchal motherhood. It is the mother's *job* to prepare the daughter for the use of men. She must teach her, by example, how to assume the terrible responsibility for maintaining the center—the stabilizing core of family and the private world. She must instruct her in the self-defeating standards of taste which will govern the daughter's attitudes toward her own body and face, her personality, and her choices of life adventures. Successful mothering is still measured in terms of the daughter's attractiveness to men, her success in a male-controlled work world, and her reproductive capacity. These successes depend to a large degree upon the daughter's ability to assimilate into male culture. She must learn to conform to the aesthetic rules which deify female youth and teach allegiance to a hierarchy which will forever divide her from other women. I do not believe that true reconciliation between women is possible until daughter-rearing goals are radically modified. The betrayal of the Daughter by her loving Mother poisons the relationships between all women, but most clearly those between young women and old women.

One of the remedial steps lesbians can take is to make a clear distinction between old lesbians and our own mothers. Another is to sort out and question the *roles* which our default assumptions tend to assign to women older or more motherly than ourselves. As Cynthia Rich points out

> If I carry in my head the notion that you are "young enough to be my daughter," or you are thinking, "she is old enough to be my grandmother," the quality of our dialogue is instantly converted. Our roles are defined for us; the possibility for real exchange between us is radically diminished." [8]

We also need to outgrow our childhood anticipation of service from women older than ourselves. Barbara Macdonald is very clear about the exploitative expectations of younger women.

> Today, the evidence is all around us that youth is bonded with the patriarchy in the enslavement of the older woman. There would, in fact, be no youth culture without the powerless older woman. There can be no leisure elite consuming class unless it is off the back of someone. The older woman is who the younger woman are better than—who they are more powerful than and who is compelled to serve them. [9]

I look back at my personal experience as a good patriarchal wife/mother with the painful wisdom of hindsight and recognize my deep collusion in the generational divisions which now afflict me. Even though my own mother was a professional woman throughout her life (reflecting the influence of the earlier wave of feminism, as well as the fact that my father was a poor provider), I fell into wifely dependency and filled the servant role for my children and husband. Like so many other women of my generation, I left a war-time job as a shipfitter to marry and become Supermom to a large family. Not only did I betray my daughters by teaching them the standards of taste learned from my mother, but I also complied with their expectations of maternal servitude, generated through an alliance with their father.

The children learned an assumption of privilege from their father, and he in turn became one of the children — legitimately passive, irresponsible. For him, the equal partnership in parenting I had expected meant giving me some help around the house when the children were young. (Even this was considered very progressive by our contemporaries.) The onus of parenting was truly mine — the children were psychologically single-parented. Not only did these circumstances infantilize an already emotionally stunted man, but my older daughters never witnessed any *exchange* of nurturance. In their view of how the world worked, mothers gave, and men/daughters received. Ours was such an isolated nuclear family that they literally never had any opportunity to witness me being nourished, sustained, taken care of, or emotionally supported. The *absence* of experience is just as effective a conditioner as repetitive experience. My older daughters, now in their thirties, are dutiful wives but still do not know how to extend nurturance to me, or to negotiate when we have a difference of interest. As Macdonald points out:

> It becomes more clear that the present attitude of women in their twenties and thirties has been shaped since childhood by patriarchy to view the older woman as powerless, less important than the fathers and the children, and there to serve them both; and like all who serve, the older woman soon becomes invisible. [10]

Only the youngest, who at twelve came with me when I escaped into the relative sanity of the lesbian world, saw me in loving and reciprocal interactions with a range of other people, including women lovers. Now only she of my three daughters is able to exchange nurturance with me; only she is relatively free of ageist interactions with me.

It is Macdonald's insight that the alliance of father with children in the exploitation of the mother helps to create ageist responses to all older women. As the Victorian authoritarian husband/father was vanquished by an earlier wave of female emancipation, men have had to re-group within the family to maintain the slave status of the woman. Demands made by children on the mother are seen to be as fully legitimate as those of the husband, if not more so. As the children grow up, they continue to relate to older women with the clear expectation of service. By then they have laid claim to a place of privilege in the power hierarchy.

Do Lesbians Really Need Old Victims?

By now it should be clear that in many ways the landscape over the crest of the hill is different from the upgrade in *degree* of intensity rather than patriarchal *content* of oppression. However, political struggles between women have focused on ethnic, racial, and class divisions. Movement women have made some small progress in diminishing these tensions, but at the same time, all of us are socialized in the ways of the Fathers. At an unthinking, irrational level, our world is still divided into those who give and those who get; those who are decided for and those who decide; those who are victims and those who victimize. This we have learned from our families and all the other power hierarchies we observed as we grew up. In the either/or victim/victimizer choice our internal need to escape the victim position transcends our raised consciousness. The choices we make whereby we become victimizers are made on the basis of default assumptions, unconscious stereotypes, adherences to standards of taste which are alien to our avowed politics. These choices are the primary inhibitors of significant political cohesion between lesbians.

Fear of contempt is the tool for social control lesbians use. Avoidance—the averted gaze—is the whip of our system. We use scapegoating and the pack behavior which we learned within our family of origin to establish and maintain power differences. Much of woman-to-woman interaction consists of automatic scanning for and assertion of the dominant position (normally occupied by the male in mixed-sex situations). First we act out of terror of being the victim. Once we establish that we are not the victim, we need to escape guilt. The Other-who-is-in-fact-one-of-us, such as the old woman or the fat woman or the disabled woman, becomes the victim—the one who is shunned, the contemptible one.

For the mid-life woman, and especially the mid-life lesbian, sexual erasure is the most urgent and emotionally devastating aspect of ageism. Middle age can be a time of desperate passing. Confidence diminishes and doubts multiply. These feelings often coincide with pressures at work which are also age related. The mid-life woman drinks the milder poisons of age prejudice every day. It is not the distilled tincture which the old woman drinks, but it is the same poison. The mid-life lesbian is also very good at serving it up to those whose years threaten her pretense of passing.

I am describing the polarized dance lesbians have learned as women, surviving in the "real" world (of compulsory heterosexuality), where many opportunities are determined by our race, looks, class, able-bodiedness, and age. In the larger culture, lesbians often reap rewards in jobs according to how we compare with other women. In our own world of power, influence, and sexuality, we maintain this comparative and judgmental hierarchy ourselves. Age is the underlying agent of change in circulating power within the class of women, robbing Garbo to pay Twiggy.

Youth provides women with a temporary illusion of opportunity in the work world. As youth is the primary requirement for the role of phallus stiffener, there are a great number of jobs for which only young women qualify. There is a chasm of identity which comfortably separates young women from women who they perceive as not passing. Old women are segregated and desexualized by both men and younger women. This attitude tends to make legitimate the assumption that all women not in that category are sexually accessible to men. "The woman who too decisively resists sexual overtures in the work place is accused of being 'dried-up' and sexless or lesbian."[11] A young woman's fear that these descriptions will be applied to *her* may reduce her will to resist unwanted sexual advances. Fear of being seen as too old to harass may lead young women to participate in the displacement of older women workers. In the competition between women for work, younger women have played scab to the struggle of older women for recognized seniority and reasonable pay.

There is a limited period of time in a woman's life when she is allowed to exert the power which masculinist values bestow upon sexual energy. My personal experience of street hassling illustrates this. As an adolescent, my need for recognition accepted any offering, even though I wondered constantly whether the whistle was for *me* — for my specialness. By seventeen, this question had found its answer. I began the long period of developing techniques of rebuff. As my body thickened and my hair grayed, there was a time when I simply forgot about harassment. Then suddenly I became aware that not only was unwanted attention absent, but my personal space — the ground ceded to me by those who passed me on the street — had shrunk. No man or woman met my eye. Through the absence of harassment, I discovered the invisibility of age. Invisibility needs to be described in all its subjective horror. It takes many forms, the most searing being its sexual form. One scarcely recovers from the ambivalence which sexual objectification evokes when one is plunged into the emotional vacuum which its withdrawal triggers.

Lesbian youth worship differs little from heterosexual youth worship. But the deprivation of sexual recognition between women which takes place after middle age (or the point when a woman no longer passes for young) includes withdrawal of the emotional work which women do to keep the flow of social interactions going: compliments, questions, teasing, touching, bantering, remembering details, checking back, supporting.

These are ethical issues which younger lesbians need to consider in their relations with older women. What do lesbians want to do about those human connections which do not directly enhance the primary goals of career or personal gratification? Are we so captive to the cultural fear of female obsolescence that we let time and indifference gradually strip women of power, work, visibility, and finally human contacts? We need to negotiate a feminist code of honor between young and old, designed for our ultimate and mutual benefit. The call for this must come from young lesbians, as well as old.

What Do Old Lesbians Really Want?

As with naming sexism in the early sixties, the first problem old women have is to establish our legitimacy when we speak out against circumstances that others have never thought to question. Whenever old women complain of ageism in a gathering of women, there are inevitably those in their late forties for whom it is important to deny the observation. "I have grown children," they testify, "so I certainly qualify as an older woman and I haven't experienced any discrimination!" It would help if women in their forties and fifties assumed that they might be suffering from a kind of perverse crisis of fear which increases their alienation from old women.

However, women of all ages have a deep investment in denying age hatred. To those lesbians who point out that they have friends whose lovers are twenty years older, I say: "But how often is that lover a woman in her sixties? How many women in their seventies are your intimates? Do you know anyone who has a close friend in her eighties?"

Ageism appears to pollute women's experience at different ages, or at different stages of physical change or disability. Some older women are able to delay aging—"outwitting Nature," it is called. Old women who are physically small, "cute," or who emanate the vibes of Daughter rather than Mother may succeed in passing far longer than their more bulky peers. They often deny other women's experiences of pain.

The way to respond to *all* accusations of ageism is identical to how we must respond to accusations of racist, classist, physicalist, or sexist behavior. This is not necessarily to say that the action or absence of action has been correctly named. Nevertheless, we must do a lot of listening, both inwardly and outwardly. Resistance, excuses or rationalizations only compound our problems. There are basic questions which fifteen years of feminism have taught us to ask: Who profits? What are the hidden assumptions? Why have we ignored it? How many of the culturally mandated attitudes have we internalized? When an old woman raises the issue of ageism, do not explain to her what you *really* meant. Listen.

Since there are so few from my side of the hill making demands or even expressing dissatisfaction, there are many who challenge me by demanding concrete examples of ageism. If I am not pressed for a story about my past, I am asked for an example which will illustrate the charges I have made. Both demands annoy me. Like most people, I am focused on my present life, not my past. I am not some walking museum of memorabilia, either camp or quaint, to be mined by others' curiosity. As for ageism, I find that I can say how it feels, or describe whom it serves, or speculate about its roots. But there is no way for me to tell stories which will illustrate the complex circumstances surrounding my losses because of ageism.

It is possible to illustrate stereotyping, but this is only

a part of the pain. Let me give an example: I came to a meeting at the home base of a country collective which published a magazine. As I greeted those I knew and found a seat, one offered me a drag from the reefer she was smoking. Without much consideration, I took a puff. This ordinary social action on my part evoked a long discharge of heavy handed approval from another woman whom I hardly knew. She was delighted to know that I smoked. She though it was absolutely wonderful. It had never occurred to her that I would indulge. On and on. The only woman in the group who found her condescension disturbing said "But Baba's a *head*!" She seemed to know that I needed *some* kind of defense, but failed in its execution.

By verbalizing a default assumption about white-haired women (one possibly shared by others in the room), my tormentor was able to set me up as Other. She happened to be a woman of color. I remember various cutting rebuttals including some with racist overtones which flashed through my mind, none of which I used. She was exercising her age dominance, and I in my discomfort mentally reached for white dominance as a defense. It is not enough that we learn not to say these things. *We have to unlearn needing to think them.* To do this, we have to build for ourselves a self-image that will not be served by these easy power gains. Such a story can forewarn women of "things not to say." But don't ask me for catchy stories which even begin to describe the righteous rejections, trashings, and betrayals which ageism has brought into my life.

When there is no regular channel for redress, I don't know what to do but call on others to hear my testimony, to share my pain, and to help clarify for me the universality of my experience. I believe that ageism does not result from fear or envy of the accumulated experience of an elder, nor is it the reflection of some primal response to the inevitable march of time toward death, despite the repeated use of these cliches in the apologies of the young. These rationalizations, like so many raised in defense of sexism, use their ranges power between women. It robs old lesbians of their rightful place of respect and equality. With all the strength of self-fulfilling prophecy, it shapes the lives of all lesbians, even the most self-defined and self-confident. It can diminish and warp us into parodies of our essential selves.

How do old lesbians want to be treated within the lesbian world? That is difficult to say. There is a kind of care which we take with women we wish to know. We give them our attention. We make allowances for their peculiarities. We monitor our own behavior for impositions or assumptions which we cannot justify to ourselves or to them. Caring treatment involves effort — emotional work well invested in the interests of friendship between women.

Let me speak for myself. First and foremost, I need lesbians with whom I can test possibilities, with whom I can exchange disagreement and anger, with whom I can be comfortably intimate — women I can trust. I need, in order to be fully sane, a circle of women who can reflect me back to myself without having to judge or chastise or control me — lesbians who can give me both resistance and validation. There is a lot of political work I can do with women who are aware of their responses, who know disagreement between us does not mean that I am bad. Also, I expect women younger than myself to acquaint themselves with issues that are important to my age bracket and include them in *their* political life. If I nurture them, they must recognize that I want to be nurtured in return. I am not asking for anything different today than what I expected fifteen years ago when I first came out.

The potential energy which is dissipated through woman-to-woman ageism may not be obvious until one gets "over the hill." But it should be clear to all lesbians that ageism distracts us from the pursuit of our essential Self, the very identity which lesbianism makes possible. Active confrontation of our conditioned loathing of the old woman is only the first step. The second is to become consciously anti-ageist, a step toward self-love, a step away from the contempt and terror with which we evade our eventual future.

33

The Politics Of Female Age

In a man, longevity seems to produce one of two results: either an extinction of his only identity through retirement, or the expansive power of the old judge or chairman or academic or mogul who dies with his boots on. The latter is the modern equivalent of attainment of godhood when finally he can do no wrong. During the scramble up the ladder, doubts and compromises may sometimes have softened his developing omnipotence. But being at the top and being old is a poisonous combination. Once there, he may never know the face of candor. He is *yes*ed without respite.

Few old women suffer personally from this syndrome, but we may be forced to observe it in the old men we know, or to absorb the great-hero-Patrimyth of the soap operas, the movies and party politics. Often we must choose between such men for high office; to them we must entrust our financial well-being; our lives rest in their bellicose hands as they manipulate military "security." If we have had a husband or a male boss, we know why they are the way they are. We have watched power erode their judgment in small significant steps as we served the male-on-the-way-up.

Yet women as a class resist the leadership or the experience of old women — almost as if they were patriarchs upon whom there were no curbs, who had secret power they could not limit. The old woman must not be listened to, must not be trusted, must not wield power, must not influence our lives, must not gain our attention. This deeply ingrained reversal of our own self-interest is ancient conditioning. Thus it is that the patriarchs have taught us to contain and defang the potential revolt which the experienced woman might ferment against him.

On the Geriatric Grab

The aging Gay and Lesbian is a subject on which very little definitive work has been done. Right now, it frightens many of those in our community. But ignoring a problem never makes it go away. Seniors can and do learn to enjoy their lifestyle. For many, and incredible as it may seem, they find it to be the happiest time of their lives.

This is a quote from a press release sent out by The Society of Senior Gay and Lesbian Citizens seeking subjects for a study. It manages, in a relatively few words, to exemplify the relationship between experts on aging and the subjects whose presence provide their livelihood, the grist for their mill.

For those whose consciousness is insufficiently elevated to detect the ageism, let me be explicit. I, an old lesbian, find that I have become a research subject–meaning a problem which is of sufficient magnitude to warrant study. A subject, a problem which one may ignore, an "it." My community, according to this press release, does not include me. It is frightened of my condition. However, lesbians can be heartened by "definitive" work on me which will show that things are not as bad as they, the community, imagines.

Any pleasure I may be experiencing in life is hard to believe, in light of this alleged condition. However, with the help of paid professionals, I can be re-educated into happiness. Presumably this study will be a comforting substitute for their ignoring me.

Growing Old In The Mainstream

Periodically I scan the *Aging* section of my local woman's bookstore, looking for something which will expand my understanding of my own circumstances. Surely as feminism trickles down from those who are refining its myriad applications, I will find something which illuminates the experience of old women or even better, old lesbians. But my life story is seldom reflected in the books I find. Even more disappointing, I do not recognize the attitudes and values purported to be common to my general age category. I believe there is an unconscious ideology maintained by the professionals who write about old women which obscures or denies the experiences we've had and choices we've made.

Lillian Rubin's study of women between the ages of thirty-five and fifty-four, coyly titled *Women of a Certain Age*,[12] is an example of this professionalized myopia. The hidden agenda of Rubin's book is to expose the continuation of female servitude within motherhood and marriage, despite the explosion of changed values and new opportunities which the past twenty years have brought. Unfortunately, her compassionate feminist scholarship is marred by heterosexist bias. The lack of examples of alternatives in life style or goals which might provide fulfillment for the older woman outside of male-controlled work or male-oriented home dilutes the impact of her message.

Rubin's interest in the subject of the mid-life woman's search for self sprang from her own herstory. After a divorce, she returned to college as a single mother. She went on to achieve professional success with the help of a supportive, atypical second husband. But most of the respondents to her study are women who cling to what they know or have, no matter how dismal, instead of stumbling out into the great adventurous unknown. "When it comes to wanting something for themselves outside the home as well as in it — to thinking about their lives and to making plans for living in some autonomous and independent way—women bear the limitations and restrictions that come with their gender, a fact of birth that settles their future, almost without question, on the day they are born."

This depressing reality, fully documented by the exhaustive questioning of 120 white women (largely residents of the San Francisco Bay Area) who "earlier in their lives, had taken marriage and motherhood as their primary life tasks," reflects a methodology limitation of the study. The sample was collected by snowballing from one respondent to another, thus automatically insuring a heterosexual and coupled bias. Also, Rubin excluded black women and widows from the group because she believed that they experienced fundamentally different mid-life transitions. (She does not mention other racial or ethnic groups.) These methodological limitations reflect in turn Rubin's unconscious ideological bias. Not surprisingly, of the target group only 22 percent were single women (a small percentage, I think, for this age bracket), and only one "was in the process of discovering herself a lesbian after having been married for 22 years." (This statement, from the Appendix, is the only use of the word "lesbian" in the book. Although the book is filled with quotes from the other women, there are no recognizable quotes from this lesbian.)

"Well, what did you expect?" you might ask. But Rubin really is trying to use her scientific sociological study to make a feminist point. From the safety of her heterosexually orthodox sample, Rubin launches into a deep critique of the individualized consciousness of mid-life women. She shows how the demands of their families—teen-age children and husbands—intersect to maintain the existing social structures of female subordination. Interweaving the plight of her respondents with her own memories, she details the resistance of the husband/child alliance to the woman's timid return to school. She describes the difficulties which a mid-life woman faces when she assumes a career path which threatens the services expected by her family. Even an empty nest does not protect her from restrictions upon her choices. Typically, she is still concerned with the male ego support needed by her husband — from faking orgasms in order to sustain his diminished sexual capacity (sometimes despite her own increasing sexual appetite), to living vicariously through him.

It is true that I learned more from Rubin's challenging interrogations of her subjects than I would have learned from most of the books of this kind written by young male gerontologists or therapists. But Rubin's questions are not as value free as she assumes. For instance, she asks: "You live your life as if you're the only one who values this marriage. Yet, your husband has lived in it for the same twenty-odd years. Don't you think he values it enough to make some accommodations to your needs at this time?" or "Do you take yourself seriously?" She also raises important questions about the credibility of the answers which women give to researchers when they find that they must admit to attitudes which do not conform to the social imperative that husband, home and family come first. Over and over Rubin reveals the defensiveness which homebound women feel toward the ideas of liberation and self-respect which have filtered through to them from the women's movement.

The respondents are women who married in the fifties and sixties, roughly the generation of the mothers of the majority of movement women. I recognize from my own experience that the service and self-sacrifice these mothers exhibit are sometimes necessary with very young children. But their docility as the nest begins to empty is less familiar. Some of these women are the mothers of feminist — even lesbian — daughters. Why is there no evidence of non-traditional pressures on them to do something about their lives while they still can? Don't women know the statistical probabilities surrounding marriage? Many are dumped for a younger woman or are widowed. They are stalked by poverty and loneliness in their old age. So why don't they choose the risks of further education, job upgrading, career change, or sexual autonomy—the kind of gambles taken by the many older lesbians I know who broke away from mid-life married stagnation.

From thirty-five on, many married women with teen-age or older children make self-defeating decisions. These life choices reflect the illusion that they will be able to live out the rest of their lives in emotional and financial security under diminished work stress. Says Rubin: "It is, after all, the triumph of the socialization process that we internalize the mandates of our culture so profoundly that we believe we are acting on inherent and individual choices." Old women are the throw-away people of our society, marginal to both the work and marriage marketplace. Motherhood has habituated them to a stance of service. But as women age, the people who use them may find their services "con-venient but expendable." Rubin clearly is concerned about this reality. Unfortunately, by choosing a sample which ex-cluded the mid-life explorations of women of color, single women who do not maintain a coupled social network, and lesbians, she may have deepened the dread and powerless-ness of many older women.

What We Take for Granted, We Cannot See

The lesbian's perspective toward aging and ageism may be more insightful than that of the heterosexual woman. It is the perspective of marginality; the view from outside the security and stagnation of such roles as wife, daughter-in-law, sister-in-law, mother-in-law, mother, grandmother, daughter. It is not that the lesbian does not fill these roles. Rather, her tenure within them is colored by the fact of her social marginality, both in her own eyes and in others'.

Centrality, as opposed to marginality, is normalcy, middle Americanness, cultural assimilation. It presses and erodes the self within. That diminution is necessary in order to sustain the integrity of the system and its values. The reward assimilation offers is a relief from doubts about direction and choices—a feeling of stability in the winds of social and technological change. Roles are the core of that safety.

It is useful to analyze the state of mind which makes "natural" and hence mandates oppressive behavior toward old women. This behavior is not noticed—it is the usual way people act without thinking. Age segregation, youth chauvinism, youth/beauty worship, age passing, revulsion for age—all express ageist attitudes which are "natural," hence invisible and politically inaccessible.

Colette Guillaumin, the French sociologist, shows how it has been possible to expose the systems and ideologies invisible to women themselves through the impact of feminist theory. She questions the distinction between theory and politics in her analysis of the effect of theory upon the relations between the sexes. She says:

> Nevertheless it is an undeniable invisibility, anchored in a commonplace fact; the belief that if things are thus, they are naturally thus and fated to remain so; therefore there is nothing particularly unusual about it, it cannot be analyzed, and there is

nothing there to be discovered or understood, since the only reason for analyzing something is to change it, to interfere with it. (Thinking already means changing. *Thinking about a fact already means changing that fact.*) It is obvious that the long-standing blindness of theory, whether psychological or sociological theory, simply resulted in attesting to belief in the natural ineluctability of these relationships. . . . In physics or mechanics, in biology or medicine, however, *it is precisely the category of natural facts that is questioned.*[13]

If theory can restructure relations as she suggests, this concept is applicable to the interactions between the generations of women. It is not enough to describe ageism by telling how the male doctor battens off the fears of old women nor how older men reject older women because their sexual conditioning leaves them dependent on young flesh. These are not subtle discoveries nor are they the core of old women's anguish. Rather it is pivotal to analyze the subjugation of the old mother by her daughter. We must acknowledge women's active participation in an invisible female power structure, the effective functioning of which depends upon age prejudice as well as inappropriate emphasis on roles. The exposed perspective of the old lesbian is often able to depersonalize and hence "de-naturalize" ageism through her conscious detachment from those roles.

Small Talk

I have not called the woman I met at Jean's party. I do not reach out. At least part of the reason for this passivity lies in my identity as a lesbian and a single woman. The woman was one of the legion of liberal, artistic, old women who abound in Northern California. They take courses, do the shit work for liberal causes, and hide their poverty behind a shield of smiling and genteel compliance. Nice liberal ladies, bent upon good works and having as good a time as possible under the circumstances.

These women are all single just like me. To my ear "single" sounds different after fifty than before. To cling to hetero-respectability when you are a fifty-five year old single woman is beyond my comprehension. There are overtones of rejection and desexualization to the word "single" when attached to an old woman which I resist. These women are, I assume, more or less celibate, just like me. What is the difference between their celibacy and mine? Their self-image and mine? Their orgasmic life and mine? I don't know, and even more frustrating, I know that there is no way for me to find out. Discussing vulnerabilities such as these is not something they would share with a lesbian.

I suffer a terrible impatience with their silence when I generalize about patriarchy or men. I am embarrassed by their deference in interactions with the wheeling-and-dealing leftist men who need their shit-work. I am enraged by the absence of a pro-woman bias, their squishy acceptance of all the commercialized spirituality and anti-feminist bullshit. Do they really believe in the integrity of the ambitious young men who lead the liberal causes they phone or walk for? Are they new to politics, or are they just so used to serving that they have forgotten how to question?

More on Small Talk

Obligatory communal eating is terribly tedious for the old woman. Now that I live alone again, away from the demands of community, I savor my escape. It is not that I don't like eating with others. For me food is a social experience, both in preparation and consumption. I miss the sound of voices, the interplay of ideas, the laughter and chatter which has always been part of my experience until now. I was never old before, you see.

Being old in a communal food setting where the average age is somewhere in the twenties is pure torture. I have grown used to the workshop or committee or affinity group where everyone is thirty years or more my junior. In these I function fairly well. Although I sometimes grow exhausted because of the absence of peers, when there is an established agenda, I am not separated as much from the other women. But eating together (or partying, which usually includes eating) means interaction unregulated by a predetermined subject. Conversation while eating depends on shared experience or interests — or the willingness to make the search for some commonality. Here ageism wipes the conversational slate clean. Other than asking me about my children, most ageist strangers assume that there can be no overlapping interest. Small talk becomes my burden of initiation and maintenance.

The communal meals at the women's land where I lived for two and a half years were typical of this problem. From the sound of the dinner bell, I forced myself to be the-one-who-I-was-not. Candles burned on our big table; the food was hot and carefully prepared by one of us; it was the only assured time we had together each day. But it had been agreed that land issues did not aid digestion, so we did not talk shop. That left conversation. The primary topic, as we ate our ideologically correct vegetarian fare, was junk food. We never allowed ourselves the luxury of really talking about ourselves or our needs. Was it because I was there that this was suppressed between us? I tried desperately to be who they wanted me to be—nice, quiet, invisible. If traveling women were eating with us, they were either tongue-tied with me, or they simply talked among themselves, as if I were not there. No one touched me, or looked me in the eye, or affirmed me with small acts of nurturance.

Even More on Small Talk

Why do we ask the question: "What do you do?" Do we really want to know if the woman we query has a high status job? Are we gauging her worth by how much she makes a week? How many women are proud of what they do? What about the old woman, the single mother on welfare, the unemployed, the woman who waits on tables or cleans houses, the student, the undertaker, the FBI agent? It is a strange question for women to ask each other. Until very recently we were not sure that we *were* somebody beyond our role attachment to a man. Now our worth is subject to male occupational terms.

"How do you make your living?" isn't much better unless we make it clear that we are exchanging information about surviving in a man's world. That is valid woman-talk. But we risk stumbling into the social chasms of "I'm just a housewife" or that Social Security is all she has. Then there are all those women who can't wait to tell you they are lawyers or doctors or electricians or carpenters or computer programmers. Is that really what we want to know?

We need some way of asking "How do you live your life?", or "What is important to you?" Our work, if any, is only a small part of how we live. Whom do we love? What are our politics? What is fun? What are the parameters of our Be/ing? How many of us know how to find out these things from an old woman? If a young woman can learn how to cross the barrier of years, then probably she will stumble less grievously with her contemporaries.

On the Language (and Politics) of Touch

I must write more about the politics of touch. I want touch, need it like a drink of water. How can it be normalized between old women and young? Touch can be a status indicator, moving down the social hierarchy, not up. The absence of touch can indicate sexual rejection, just as its presence signals interest. What sign tells another woman that we want to exchange touch, but not sex?

I have met old women who did not want to be touched. I do not know whether they never liked exchanging touch, or whether, out of a sense of shame, that refusal came with age into their vocabulary of self-inflicted deprivations.

A woman's casual touch experience changes with age. Men and most lesbians don't touch old women because they are afraid of being misunderstood. The language of touch carries complex messages of sexuality as well as friendship. Touch communicates relative power or status interlocked with sexual politics. Since an old lesbian is perceived as a non-participant in these realms, it becomes easier simply not to touch her at all. The language of touch—like other non-verbal languages such as eye contact or how we spend our time—gradually becomes a source of anxiety for the old woman, then an unexpected exchange, and sometimes finally an unwanted exchange.

As I experience these changes in my interactions with others, I must remind myself not to hate myself, not to loathe the changes in my body, not to envy the power of youth. If I project my pain onto others—wrapping myself in the small comfort of pride—then I will recoil from whatever opportunities for touch come my way. Touch is not a fringe benefit of youth, it is a human necessity.

I mentally leaf through my experiences, back to the time when I had lived in a woman's community. I remember coming home from the hospital, convalescing from a cervical cancer operation. My body was traumatized by the knife and my psyche by the drugs. I needed comfort. When

I asked the women who surrounded me to help heal me by touch, each woman had an excuse. One was feeling too annoyed with me, she said. She took great pride in being able to get in touch with her feelings. Another questioned the correctness of giving me a massage which I could not return. She was a great believer in political correctness. I grew ashamed of being a beggar and asked no more.

That memory led to others. I sifted through my inner card file of friends, thinking about our touching interactions. There is Nadine, half my age, whose touch often takes the form of mussing me up with enthusiastic abandon. She attacks my distance and shyness with the sureness of a friend who knows me well. Her touch robs me of my dignity—a blessed loss. Although she often touches me in outrageously sexual ways, it is without sexual implications. She is making a joke. When we talked once about how she would feel if the energy between us became sexual, she panicked. "What would I do?" she gasped in real alarm, just as if she were a heterosexual.

Then there is Olive, almost my age, whose recoil from *my* touch is matched only by her stiff withholding of any physical contact with me. I often stand beside her, aching with the need to hug her, to smooth her ruffled feathers, to ask for the affection I know she feels for me. She has explained that she never liked being touched by anyone, all her life, except sexually. Since she says she cannot imagine being my lover, this excuses her, I suppose.

The language of touch is so complicated! My lesbian daughter and I spent hours discussing the possible meanings of a touch to the head, as a result of this incident. I was riding in the back seat of her car, while she drove her lover Alice to where her truck was parked. Encumbered with many bags and bundles, Alice was flustered and un-centered. She was talking *at* my daughter more than to her, but in a loving and vulnerable way, while my daughter concentrated on traffic problems. I, feeling affection for Alice, reached forward and ruffled the back of her hair a little.

The touch I gave was meant to communicate empathy and sympathy, a response to her complaints and confusion. She turned and smiled at me, saying, "I'm afraid my hair hasn't been washed for a while."

When we left her at her truck, I asked my daughter why my affectionate touch had triggered that response from her. The last thing I had wanted to do was remind Alice of an imagined failing—to evoke emotions of inadequacy.

She said Alice had reacted as she would have to her own mother—that interactions between Alice and her mother were often clouded by invasive suggestions or implied criticism on her mother's part, followed by guilty evasion on Alice's part. Having confirmed my intuition that the exchange with me was ageist, she went on to describe her own responses to having her head touched by a stranger. At that time, she worked at a non-traditional job where the presence of a woman was terribly threatening to the men. They dealt with their insecurities by treating her like a mascot, including occasional pats on her head. When she tried to describe this to me, she held her head on both sides and expressed her revulsion by a wiping motion, as if she were erasing unwanted touch there as well as on other parts of her body. Her intensity was painful.

I realized that ruffling hair is something we do to children; that we touch them a lot on their heads because that is what is nearest to our hands. Touch between me and younger women is an important problem for me. What would I be saying, I wonder, if I mussed Nadine's hair like she does mine?

Youth Addiction

A group of women were talking together about our lives. I found myself forced to defend my statement that one loses friends as one gets old. One of the women countered briskly that the opposite was true for her. She had made more friends in the last four years as a lesbian than she had in the previous ten as a married woman. I countered with annoyance, "Yes, and how old are you? Thirty-eight, going on thirty-nine?" This triggered an explosion of anger in the group. I was accused of being hurtful and ageist.

"Having fewer people in your life is one of the realities of growing old."[14] As I fought back against the general consensus that my problem was personal, that I was trying to guilt-trip them, that I was misinformed — one of the women came over and touched me. She patted me in a hearty way and told me how good it was that we could go at it like this. She had never touched me before, nor has she since. In the condescension of that moment, when she asserted her dominance more clearly with touch than she had with words, I realized what was happening to me.

Too much of our self-worth seems to depend upon who or what we are not. Not only can a male feel good that he is not a woman but he is self-confident only if no one treats him *as if* he were. An alcoholic maintains self-esteem by denying addiction. Being a drunk instead of a social drinker is a terrible loss of social acceptability. An alcoholic invests exaggerated self-esteem in this denial of reality.

Twice I have lost friends who were alcoholic by raising the issue of their alcoholism with them. In both instances, I was rejected as well as abused by them verbally. Professionals who work with alcoholics say that this is common behavior in addicts when they feel their irrationally-based self-esteem threatened.

There is an analogy here to what happens when I try to to articulate my experience as an old woman to mid-life women. They are not old. Nor do they believe that they are addicted to youth or prejudiced against old age, being already in a category which suffers from ageism. I attack their self-esteem when I ask that they not counter my testimony, when I refuse to join them in their illusion.

Differences

Being the oldest in any group of women (my experience about ninety-nine percent of the time) means that I bear their combined projections of denial of aging. Fear and guilt vie for ascendancy in their unconscious. Often the women closest to my age are my primary tormentors. They take the therapeutic approach to age. This is a social worker stance which says: "Now, don't give in. The only way to stay young is to *feel* young!" Those who need this protection from their fears treat me with great cheeriness. It feels like the condescension which accompanies the self-congratulation of altruism. I am told, "No, you can't slow up. We deny you permission to be less active, less self-reliant, less nurturing of *us* than you have always been." I sometimes need to talk about the greater pain I feel in walking or sitting in the same position for a long time, as in driving a car. My middle aged friends meet this with the distancing of the therapeutic approach. Unless I insist, my friends do not accommodate themselves to my slower gait when they walk with me. Instead of the real communication of caring, the reassurance of acceptance which I seek, they give me dietary advice, podiatry suggestions and enthusiastic recommendations of their latest alternative healing experience.

One of the primary complaints of age is touch deprivation. I suspect that this problem is even more acute in the lesbian community, where the implications of touch between women have been eroticized. Physical gestures of compassion and comfort between women deeply separated by age (and, by implication, erotic potential) are uncommon. Physical playfulness and the easy touch of shared identity are rare between old women and the dominant age of the feminist movement — women in their twenties and thirties. I have permission to touch, but I am not touched in return. Sometimes I interpret this as evidence of an unconsciously perceived power differential. In patriarchal body language, contact is always initiated by the more powerful.

Sometimes I experience it as sexualized rejection or revulsion. Am I the beggar at the banquet because I am the age of their mothers, isolated in proxy taboo and resentment?

Surely there is a place of right action somewhere between over-solicitous behavior and neglectful indifference. Must we choose between being the girl scout who helps the old woman across the street she didn't want to cross, and the person who rides seated before the ninth-month bulge of a woman clinging to the bus-strap above her? I am white haired and wrinkled but at the same time I am active and a hard worker. Why is it not politically correct for able-bodied women in their twenties through forties to offer me their chair, rather than watch me shift in pain on the bare floor through a meeting? Is it really true that it is up to me, that I must ask each time? Compassionate responsibility has not been named politically correct.

More accurately, others do not see me shift and squirm on the floor. They do not see me at all, or only through a fog of age-difference.

Another Difference

I love it when a new meaning to an old word gallops into my vocabulary. Take the computer terminology which is beginning to enliven common language. "Default" in computer language is the preset value chosen from the various parameters built into the programming. These values are picked because they are assumed to be the most used, the most likely to meet the needs of a secretary using the machine. The default line spacing in a word processing program is single space. If you want to double space, you have to change the default value to two. Before getting my computer, my primary experience with a default was not being able to make the balloon payment on the ranch mortgage. It was not a word I played with.

Now I can tease the concept of negative default assumptions into new associations. We women have the toggle switch set to off to so many possibilities. We do not consider them because we have been preset to a limited identity — woman. If this is true, then what about the limits which are pre-set in other identities — class or age, for instance.

I interpret much of my experience through the filter of my primary "state of emergency"— age. I watch my younger friends do the same thing, except their "primary states of emergency" are class or race or disability or body weight. Like my friend Nora. Nora is a lesbian, white, of South American ruling class origins, in her middle thirties, with a full motherly figure. Her identity — her "primary state of emergency"— is working-class Third World.

When I asked Nora how her new job with the feminist collective was going, she seemed pleased with things generally, but complained that there were class problems that were going to have to be resolved within the group. Curious, I pressed her to be more specific. "For example," she said, "everyone drinks coffee all day long, and leaves their cups around the store or in the sink. I do not drink coffee, but I like to use the sink for other things, and I can't stand the mess, so

I find myself washing coffee cups over and over. This would not happen to me except from middle-class women, who are used to having someone clean up after them."

I laughed so hard I felt forced to explain. "If it had happened to me — and it often does — I would assume that it was because they all saw me as their mother. It is not a function of class that the younger woman expects the older woman to wait on her, to pick up after her, to nurture her."

Old, Not Other

Feminists have approached the issues of female aging and old age with reluctance. For many women, resistance to the life solutions modeled by their mother's generation embodies their politics. Young liberated women hope to carve a new female identity that escapes the traps of the past. It is not a popular position to acknowledge that they will grow older, that their rejection of the past may not free them, that their mothers are not the enemy. Confronting ageism means more tiresome internal work, digging out those reliable and reassuring indicators of youthful superiority. Better to leave old women to the gerontologists.

But feminist scholarship has uncovered the *repetitive* quality of woman's resistance down through the years. We are beginning to recognize that rejection of knowledge about the lives of the preceding generation of women is part of the problem. Feminists, like everyone else, act from a socially conditioned view of female aging. That view reflects values contradictory to women's interests. The irrational loathing and terror of female aging casts a long shadow, influencing the choices of women of all ages. By dividing the generations, ageism robs women of the continuity of identity necessary for successful feminist resistance. Analysis of the historical sources of woman-directed ageism, as well as documentation of how it impacts on women's self image and life experience, is now beginning to emerge.

A recently published book brings a new perspective to this long ignored direction. Susan Hemmings's *A Wealth of Experience*[15] is a collection of life stories of a number of British women between forty and sixty-five, of varying class and ethnic backgrounds. It is an important book, not for the profundity of the material, but because it provides personal testimony which gives information about the last half of women's lives. Hemmings retains the integrity of their voices by interviewing them and then returning their words to them for editing and amplification. Almost all the pieces describe mid-life changes these women made in their lives, fueled by the impatience they felt about their service to others. Often these bursts of independence were thwarted by new demands for caretaking from husbands, parents or grown children. Some women escaped into new relationships (several becoming lesbians), new careers, new educational directions. Some maintained their marriages with mutual growth and love between partners. Repeated evidence of the adaptability of women is woven through their observations and reminiscences — adaptability demanded by changes in their roles and the deep economic unpredictability of their lives.

As these life descriptions show, the path of self-fulfillment for women is hard to identify, much less to follow. These women, like each generation since, tended to exaggerate the potential efficacy of their choices as they launched their adult lives. Often they made irreversible personal (and hence political) decisions which determined their relationship to such issues as autonomy, sexuality, or work — such as marrying to escape parents, or working instead of getting an education. Speaking for the women, Hemmings says in her introduction, "Many of our mothers, too, remembered tough fights, for the vote, for equal pay, for contraception. But despite everything, we slid into the same traps which had caught them, and lost confidence in ourselves as separate and autonomous people."

Though the lives the women lived were very different, there is thematic material which runs through their stories: marriage, being pulled in many directions, the endless necessity of upgrading their skills and education, or simply the experience of "keeping on going despite everything." As they look back, a few of the choices which these mature women identify as traps include immigration, working in order to educate others, staying in marriage out of fear of poverty, merging their earnings with their husband's, and maintaining the exterior illusion of contentment instead of showing their true feelings. Almost none were able to articulate the ageism they experience although there is some candor about their fears of growing old.

Although all but two of the women are in their middle years, Hemmings points out that they are seen as "older women," the same label that is used for their mothers' and grandmothers' generations. Women in this country who became active feminists in the 1960s are now identified the same way. Older than whom? Who defines the norm? When I organized CR groups for "older women" in the late 1960s, they were for women thirty or over. Although the majority of feminist activists may still be under thirty, the movement is now much older. The several generations of "older women" cannot be merged. Nor should we old feminists be expected to limit our interests to those problems specific to our age category. Surely the experience of old women is an important source of feminist insight, especially when we lament that our "liberated" daughters are making some of the same mistakes we did. Yet even older women, as Hemmings testifies, are "not used to anyone taking an interest, or in believing we have anything worthwhile to say about the world."

Ageism screens communication between young and old women like a one-way mirror — the old can see the young, aided as they are by memories of their own youth, but the young cannot — or will not — see their future in old women. Sensing that vital information may be hidden on the other side of the mirrored surface, the young press their faces against the barrier, only to scan their own reflections nervously for the imperfections of age. The old, on the other side, watch with sadness, recognizing their own denial of aging in the young women's faces. Why is this separation of identity between the generations so intense in women? Is it simply that postmenopausal women are seen as slipping out of those two male-defined reasons for female existence, sex object and nurturer? "Old woman" is a pejorative label; it is also a social category surrounded by taboo. The historical and symbolic roots of the this irrational state of affairs are the subject of *The Crone*.[16]

Barbara Walker, whose indefatigable research gave us the *Women's Encyclopedia of Myths and Secrets*,[17] has focused in *The Crone* on the third aspect of the Triple Goddess, the original Trinity of pre-patriarchal times. The Virgin had the power of Creation. The Mother had the gift and the power of Preservation. The Crone, whom Walker identifies as that aspect of the all-powerful Mother who embodied "the fearful potential for rejection, abandonment, and death" was the Destroyer, the one who guided the soul through the periods of non-being.

The first two aspects of the Goddess represented functions and allegiances that needed to be appropriated into the service of the newly transcendental male god. However, the concept of cosmic balance through renewal — cyclic decay and rebirth — was antithetical to the male obsession with control. The power of the Christian church rested on the doctrine of reward or punishment. Death could be defeated through correct or incorrect living. One could expect to be elevated to a static heaven or descend to an eternal hell — both defined and controlled by the priests. Walker shows how the great archetypes of the Virgin and the Mother were consolidated into the Christian figure of Mary, but the feared archetype of female age, the Crone, was eradicated. At the psychological level, the Crone symbolized the potential of infant abandonment which is the primal fear of all humans. Thus the "wise, willful, wolfish Crone" was female power and danger in its most potent form. In patriarchy she had to be erased.

Walker builds her figure of the Crone out of tiny shards of information collected from a mountain of library research. She assembles these bits and pieces of ancient information into a fascinating reconstruction of the cosmological and psychological significance of this archetype of female age. Walker does not confine her analysis to the impact of this image on women alone. The Crone, under one name or another, was part of the mythology of people from eastern Asia to Ireland, from Scandinavia to Northern

Africa. In Christian Europe, she suffered the most complete obliteration; the persecution of her earthly representatives was carried to the greatest extremes in the burning times. Walker builds a strong case that the ageism and social rejection which limits old women today is one of the most persistent legacies of that erasure.

> Patriarchal man wishes woman to continue playing the part of the unpaid, but tirelessly devoted nurturer, long after its biological foundation has crumbled, and after he ceases to grant her even the specious significance of a sex object. One reason is that patriarchal man must deny woman the essential later-life functions she naturally assumed in prepatriarchal societies: healer, judge, wisewoman, arbiter of ethical and moral law, owner of the sacred lore, mediator between the realms of flesh and spirit, and—most of all—the functions of the Crone: funerary priestess and Death Mother, controlling the circumstances of death as she controlled those of birth. In their anxiety to deny the Crone archetype through religious imagery, patriarchal societies even denied the fact of death itself.[18]

It is significant to me that old women of power are not only invisible in the present patriarchal world, but also in the feminist world which women are trying to mold from woman-defined identities and ethics. For most people, old women are still linked with death, but they are not empowered by this connection—only avoided. Even feminist women collude in denying the old woman a position of dignity and influence befitting her practical knowledge. If it is true, as the testimony of the women in Hemmings' book implies, that women have greater difficulty with nay-saying to other people's needs before menopause than after, the archetype Crone with her " 'evil eye' of sharp judgment honed by disillusioning experience" needs to be integrated into the feminist model of female identity. We need to reinvent the image of powerful, rebellious old women.

Both Britain and United States have a separate feminist movement for older women—the Older Women's League in the U.S. and the Older Feminists Network in London. These groups focus on the primary crises of age: poverty, isolation, abuses of the medical/caretaking industry, and legislative or regulatory indifference to old women. Most of the younger women involved in these organizations are geriatric workers with a professional interest in the funding of services for the aged. Although it should not be impossible to be both a feminist and a gerontologist, the two do not seem to coincide with any regularity. There has been a great silence about woman-to-woman ageism. The issues specific to female age have never been incorporated into any feminist list of the twenty most needed changes. A mutually beneficial dialogue between the generations of women is still in the future.

As a result of this separation, feminist theory has not developed an adequate model of the female life cycle. Without this, old women find themselves stereotyped as Other—old fashioned, ugly, apolitical, powerless among women, invisible—just as the patriarchs hoped when they eradicated the Crone. Walker points out that "the mind of a postmenopausal woman is virtually uncharted territory." For instance, how much information have women exchanged about the "nest-destroying" instinct in the postmenopausal woman—an internal need for "withdrawal from the abundantly other-directed behavior patterns of her mothering period, into a more self-directed mode of life"?

Our society lacks the symbolic expression of such subversive possibilities. Even feminists seem unaware of them. Yet, judging by the testimony of many of the women in Hemmings's book as well as my personal experience, female old age provides excellent potential for radical change and self-expression. But this is possible only if we are not trapped in dependent poverty; only if we learn how to resist the perennial demands which devour our energies. We also need to know that we, with our newly found independence, are accepted as allies and equals in the feminist world.

Witch Killing

It is mid-morning prime time for the preschool viewers on educational television. The program is a charming rebuttal to the warring robots which fill the cartoons on other channels. A motherly artist tells a simple fable about a miller and a goosegirl while illustrating her story with chalk drawings magically created before our eyes. The story line goes something like this. The natural good looks of the hero deteriorate. His nose gets long and pointed. Even worse, the girl who takes care of the geese disappears. A goose claims her identity. These two unfortunates join forces to decide that their troubles are caused by an old woman. They follow her when she goes into the forest to gather mushrooms, assaulting her as she talks to herself in the moonlight. After the young miller knocks her down, a bolt of lightning out of a cloud zaps her and her body disappears. The goose, now a pretty girl, and a short-nosed miller walk hand in hand into the happy-ever-after. One can be sure that nowhere are there protests being organized against this programming.

Yet I and other old women live with the social conditioning of that story in our lives, over and over again. Let me list some of the characteristics of the images which program people's responses to old women. The evil attributed to her is almost always gratuitous, without rational motivation. Care is taken to show that she is socially isolated, without friends even of her own kind. Not only is she ugly, but she causes ugliness in others—deformities, stupidities or criminal behavior. Her power to do evil is supernatural, unlike the strength or intelligence which others display in overcoming her. Above all, the violent and often treacherous means of her defeat need no justification. They are decreed by God.

Symbolic disempowerment of the potential matriarch is not limited to Grimm's fairy tales, or my experience. Rich old women are favorite targets of murder in mysteries.

In real life, old women, as they are dying, are the victims of medical technology—kept alive to fill hospital beds profitably. Old women's bodies subsidize the nursing-home industry. The old widow, poor and no longer useful or needed, is the raw material of bag ladies, or the disoriented women warehoused in mental institutions, or the isolated eccentrics with thirty cats.

Centuries have intervened since there were old matriarchs who could have threatened the power of the patriarchs. Yet the conditioning against the possibility of powerful, respected, or influential old women continues. As Barbara Walker says:

> The real threat posed by older women in a patriarchal society may be the "evil eye" of sharp judgment honed by disillusioning experience, which pierces male myths and scrutinizes male motives in the hard, unflattering light of critical appraisal. It may be that the witch's evil eye was only an eye from which the scales had fallen.[19]

The women still too young for the fate designated for the old woman often become her executioner. In my experience, I provoke the Witch killer instinct in women when I exert power in my own behalf. In a group from which I recently resigned, I was found to be the cause of the eventual demise of the whole group, months after I had left. Casting a spell which outlived my physical presence, my absence kept them from fulfilling their purpose. I had given as a reason for leaving the group that after two years I did not feel that we were capable of accomplishing the task we had assigned ourselves. I needed to move on—to find new outlets for my energy and creativity. Every unresolved problem within the group congealed into recriminations against me. I was found to be the cause of the problems which afflict others. I must be disempowered, isolated. My defeat was of such mythic and psychological significance that it justified behavior ordinarily outside the ethics of the woman's community.

It is valuable to be reminded of the historical roots of this behavior. Walker points out that

> Witches became universal scapegoats. When anything went wrong, the weather turned bad, crops failed, houses burned, wagons broke, lightning struck cows or wells went dry, the cry of witchcraft was raised. When children became disturbed or hysterical, it was demonic possession caused by a witch. All the common troubles of the human condition were attributed to witches during the persecution centuries.[20]

Disempowering the old woman is often accomplished in small increments as she ages through the withdrawal, bit by bit, of her reputation and credibility.

On Being Cursed

Twice within the last year I have had the experience of being called old to my face, with loathing and contempt. Even as I proudly took "old" into my self-definition in conscious resistance to the feared power of the word, I was unprepared for my own responses to "old" used as an expletive.

There have been many minor incidents which serve to illustrate the confusion surrounding my newly assumed identity. I read of a group of women who wanted to put out an anthology on age. They called themselves mid-life and older women. I chuckled. When I saw a magazine for women over forty, my imagination leaped to create the perfect journal for the *other* category, women ten to forty. I worried about how the woman of eighty could differentiate herself from me, if I at sixty-eight usurped the word "old." Any woman who could have birthed me is a different generation from me. Clearly, the word was hopelessly malleable, adjusting itself without resistance to the user's intent. "Old" is never used authentically, even by the eighty year old. Only as an insult does it touch deep.

Both times that men have used "old" as an oath to batter me, I was resisting their attempts to control my behavior. My town, like most others in these days of federal budget cuts, has a good number of mentally-ill people whom the authorities allow to be free as long as they are medicated. This particular man had wandered far from the village streets where he is known and tolerated to the rural lane on which I live. Finding himself out of matches for his cigarette after the sun had gone down, he began wandering the backyards. Where there was light showing, he pressed his face to the window to ask for what he needed. Unknown to me, two neighbors had already called the police before he wandered to my window.

When this disheveled, glassy-eyed man startled me by leaning in my open window, I shouted at him to get out of my yard and back onto the road. He argued. I threatened him with the police. He grew very angry and shouted: "Look, old woman, I am not doing anything wrong!" Righteously, he had reached for the word which he believed could equalize us: he, trespassing, disoriented, needy; I, old and therefore powerless, contemptible, subject to control.

The other encounter was with a veterinarian whom I challenged to adhere to the agreement his office had made with me. When I asserted my rights, I became, in his words, "a nasty little old lady." Both incidents triggered in me a rush of adrenalin out of all proportion to the provocation. I am a well-conditioned woman—usually contained and slow to anger. Instead of throwing a book of matches out the window, I called the police. On the veterinarian I unleashed a shouted string of gutter expletives which left both of us stunned.

On Speaking Out About Ageism

Twice I have tried to express myself about ageism to large gatherings of feminist women. Once was at a summer camp for lesbians. Most women used the camp as a respite from their work and relationship hassles. The camp provided a patina of consciousness raising in the form of workshops, making the fun and games more politically correct.

There I met a woman in her fifties who was spending most of her vacation week hiding in her cabin to escape the exclusion and indifference she had encountered. "I know a great many of the women here," she complained to me. "I work at the Woman's Center and they come through there, so I get a chance to get acquainted with them at the desk. I end up doing a lot of things they need done. But here they say hello and that's all."

My new friend was missing even the political workshops because of the misery of her invisibility. I knew I should do something, but what? Toward the end of the week there was an open-mike meeting. Testimonials were expected. So I testified about what I and my friend had experienced. Before I could get back to my seat, a mid-life member of the camp collective was using the mike to deny the possibility that ageism could be a problem in their camp. She knew this because she had never seen it happen, nor had it ever happened to her.

Another encounter was at a goddess conference. It was in a big auditorium at a large college, organized by academic women interested in women's spirituality. There were many presentations of the remarkable information being rediscovered by feminist scholarship about Goddess worship in ancient times, and the revival of Goddess awareness in the '70s. Although the slides of ancient Goddess figures were multi-racial and varied in body type — and included Crones — the slides of current drawings and sculpture were white, thin young Hollywood starlet type goddesses. I was furious.

Again I took advantage of an open mike. Again I was attacked by those in charge. Again women in their forties and fifties used their age to invalidate my criticism. My white hair did not suggest to them the possibility of a valid perspective different from theirs.

I have sat in many a feminist gathering as women of color, or Jewish women, or disabled women have tongue-lashed those responsible for alleged exclusion from the speakers panel or insensitivity in arrangements. But I dare not learn from these brave political examples. My case is different. I can write letters to feminist organizations demanding attention for the issues and perspective of old women. But public complaints touch the raw nerve in women called "mother telling me what to do."

A Different Kind of Love Quarrel

Within the circles of love which I draw on the map of my life are two women. Only my inner eye knows that their circles overlap. One is Nadine, friend but not lover; the other, daughter of my flesh but not friend. They are the same age. I need both of them in my life (show me the one who does not need love!). But there is always a price to pay for intimacy, and sometimes the price is too high.

When I escaped the cocoon of marriage, I started to refuse the interactions usual between a mother and a grown daughter. All lesbians must emerge through the closely-knotted sieve of our past, even our past as mothers. I had done more than come out. I had learned to demand parity in my relationships. No more playing mama. No more covert control, in *either* direction. For me, re/membering my Self meant erasure of the accommodating, self-sacrificing facade of mother. If it has been hard for me, it has been even harder for others, most especially for the daughter I no longer call my friend.

It may be that Nadine and I were both substituting each other for family. Nadine's mother, a deeply traditional and possessive woman, could not accept Nadine as a lesbian any better than *my* daughter could accept the changes lesbianism had made in *her* mother. The loss of a mother is as devastating as the loss of a daughter. Both of us must have been making unconscious replacements. Neither of us sought the old roles of family, only the commitments and forgiveness that make up the security of a circle of love. Staying linked to old lovers is a more usual path to ensuring these circles in one's life. But Nadine and I were never lovers, only friends.

Tests of these bondings often involve quarreling. When ex-lovers remain close, at least some quarrels have been survived, some differences transcended. Nadine and I blundered into such a test. It was centered around a trip we had planned to take together. Originally we had expected to drive in my car from the Bay Area to Los Angeles, where we both had relatives to visit. As the time for the trip drew near, I encountered a series of negative omens, culminating in a near auto collision. Was I being warned to postpone the trip? I turned to the *I Ching* for needed clarity. The archaic language of the reading was more explicit than usual: "The horse and wagon will part, there will be bloody tears, nothing should be undertaken. Further, the superior woman should be careful of her words."

When I told Nadine of my fears and the words of the reading, suggesting delay, she said that I should ask the same question of the *I Ching* again when I was less upset. Such heretical advice shocked me. Then she announced that she would fly down alone, adding that she might drive back with me. What I heard was a lack of support and a withdrawal of nurturance. What she had heard was incipient control — the mother's voice. The substance of the quarrel which erupted was insignificant compared to our sound and fury. Nadine stomped and yelled, her voice octaves higher with righteous indignation. Challenged by her obvious ease in fighting, I managed to shout an insulting rebuttal. If we were competing in the art of verbal battery, she outclassed me. At no point in the quarrel did I remember to be careful of my words.

If only I could have spoken without haste and said:

> There is a difference between the way we are listening. You use, as an example of your alleged nurturance of me, that you listen to my "tales of woe." I listen to yours too. The difference lies in the fact that it never occurred to me that listening was just an act of nurturing. I listen for my own use. I pick through your haystack, looking for a needle of insight. Your experience becomes mine. I chew it, digest it, make it into my concept body.
>
> There is another difference between your listening and mine. Nothing that you tell me about your marriage, your insecurities, your love life, your ambitions, is intrinsically unknown to me. Do not feel in-

sulted by that fact, because it is both true and false, like all facts. Your experience is at once unique and painfully familiar. The difference is that it happened in 1975, not in 1945 when I was your age. Focusing on the sameness is possible for me. Comparison between the times is possible for me. Comparisons between personal differences at the same age are possible for me. Comparison between your lesbian consciousness and my then-straight consciousness is possible. All this gives me a whole range of equations to solve that you do not have.

What are my "tales of woe"? I talk about my problems with my grown children, my shortages of lovers, all the encounters I sustain which lack the easy lubricant of youthful sexuality, the oppression of my invisibility. What can you know of these? It is as if I were describing my experiences homesteading on Mars. Somewhere inside of you, you are reassuring yourself that you have sense enough not to *try* to homestead on Mars. How do I know that? Because that is what I thought at your age.

After we were calm again, Nadine said: "I feel you are detached from me." Again I failed her. Had I been more swift, more sure, I would have found the words. I needed to reassure her and, at the same time show the damage.

Listen, Nadine, these troubles between us are lessons in bonding. We found each other following an Ariadne's thread so tenuous that both of us deserve black belts in witchery. Now we are learning to listen to the slippery clean sound of that web which binds us. We both know that what we are doing is important.

When we were quarreling, it came as a total surprise to both of us when I burst into tears. A great wave of anguished helplessness — those body signals of childhood — swept around me. "YOU MUST CONTROL YOURSELF—YOUR BOWELS, YOUR BLADDER, YOUR EMOTIONS! SEPARATE OFF! SEPARATE OFF!" roared one angry voice inside me. And another cried, "GET OUT! LEAVE ME! YOU ARE ON YOUR OWN!" There it was, child-daughter to an angry mother and angry

70

mother to a child-daughter, in one internal dialogue. Nadine was wrong to think that the old terrors our quarrel was evoking were exclusively hers. It was at this point in the quarrel that we both had sense enough to refuse the inner shielding which always lies so dangerously handy to one's fears. We talked.

Instead of ending our friendship, the quarrel proved to be a necessary foundation. Between us, we sorted out some of the old expectations we had brought, like rusty keepsakes, to our friendship. We discovered, for instance, that her difficulties with listening came from lessons she had learned from her father. Nadine remembered how he discounted, or trivialized her mother's talk, or took her nurturing for granted. Our models of how to interact with women older than ourselves were hopelessly marred. We hadn't seen our mothers nourished or emotionally sustained, nor had I been nurtured within the family I mothered. Nurturing the nurturer, like assertiveness, is not taught to women. Even worse, our mothers did not instruct us how to exert legitimate self-interest without manipulating people.

The tension of our quarrel was caused by the withdrawal of nurturance (hers) and being controlling (mine). We shared the motivation to overcome our fear of betrayal and feel trust for each other. Betrayal and trust—the opposite sides of the coin of intimacy—the currency we were exploring. Nadine had forged her personal identity by escaping the control of her mother of birth. But if I said to Nadine: "*I* do not need to control you. You do not have to assert your autonomy with *me!*" then I must probe anxiously my conditioning as a mother—I must be sure.

A close and reciprocal friendship between a young and an old woman is not easy to negotiate. I believe that when lesbians fall in love, our bodies create an imitation of the amniotic union between daughter and mother before birth. We have triggered the blissful body knowledge of Oneness. (The male fetus is identical to his mother's flesh for only the first five weeks before testosterone differentiates him, but the female chemical union lasts for the full nine months.) I never had the courage to talk to Nadine about these ideas because we are not lovers. As it was, we stumbled about in the rubble of our mothering experiences without the aid of that amniotic imitation. Without the quarrel, our connection would never have been intense enough to endure as a circle of love.

On Becoming Old Women

When we ask for a chance to live our old age in comfort,
creativity and usefulness, we ask it not for ourselves alone, but
for you. We are not a special interest group. We are your roots.
You are our continuity. What we gain is your inheritance.
Irene Pauli, *Some Ironies of Aging*

How can old women define age and ageism so that false understanding of these subjects does not dominate the interactions between women, keeping us separate? Aging is a natural and universal personal experience which begins the day we are born. It is a process of challenge — not necessarily growth and development when we are young as opposed to loss and deterioration when we are old — but learning through change. Ageism is the negative social response to different stages in the process of aging and is a political issue. The ageism which old women experience is firmly embedded in sexism — an extension of the male power to define, control values, erase, disempower and divide. Woman-to-woman ageism is an aspect of the horizontal conflict which usurps the energies of the colonized — part of the female competition for the crumbs of social power.

How can the same word be used for the experience of teen-agers, old women, and the most powerful men in the world? Yet we say that all these are subject to *ageist* attitudes — stereotyping and denigration because of age. But each age group — children, teens, mid-life women, old women, old men — have radically different expectations of their due — their rightful social place. For an old woman, ageism is a killer because her sense of worth has been inexorably eroded by a lifelong pursuit of youth/beauty.

Age passing — passing for young enough — is part of all female experience. The foundation of lies built into passing and the fear and loathing of female aging keep the generations of women — decade by decade — divided from each other. Age passing is one of the primary learning arenas of female competition, as well as an apprenticeship in hatred

73

of old women. When we pass easily, we gain comfort knowing that we do not have to identify with the woman who, in our view, is not passing. "I am not like her" translates easily into "I am better than her." In our thirties we do not want to be mistaken for forty. In our forties we do not want anyone to assume we are fifty. Somewhere in the fifties, anxieties about the increase in rejection and invisibility become critical. This is often a time when our trained inability to identify with women older than ourselves reaches its climax. Old women cannot rely upon mid-life women as allies. The mid-life woman in her rage and fear may unconsciously discharge all kinds of covert aggression against the personification of what threatens her — the old women.

Can women afford to ignore issues which surround the aging process? When I asked younger women what they thought ageism was all about, they talked about the aura of death and decay which permeates age for them, the oppressive power/over of the mythic Mother figure, and the deplorable neglect exhibited by the authorities in making adequate institutional responses to age. None have seen ageism as a problem of prejudice or bigotry on their part. With the righteousness of a news anchorman, most of my informants advocated better government support for the old. But government subsidies for medicine and institutional care have created a highly profitable industry of geriatric technology, with the elderly aid recipients captive to the modern Grail, longevity. Just staying alive is a false goal. Acceptance of age in women has not kept pace with our increased life expectancy. It is the *quality* of that extra time that is important. As long as women allow themselves to be brainwashed into worshiping youth and plasticized beauty, increased life expectancy (and the institutionalized responses to it) will remain a burden for both the young and the old.

How can ageism be defined by women? How can we develop a clear vocabulary and theory? Can we afford to ignore it? For me these questions are more than rhetorical. I am an old woman living in a highly politicized community of women. I find struggle and change taking place in relation to all the differences between women except age. I need to divert some of that political consciousness toward ageism.

I am an *old* woman. I am sixty-eight. Part of the reason I self-identify as *old* is a need to escape the prissy category of older. This label is used for women from eighteen to eighty, depending on the age and consciousness of the user. I once wore a button which said, "I like older women." When a young man accosted me in a supermarket to ask where he could get a button just like mine, I realized that *his* older woman was probably twenty-three. But what are my choices? I get called "little lady" by strangers, although I am neither. I found that the decision to abandon the tag "older woman" was easier than claiming the identity of *old*. *Old* was without hope, ignored, invisible, trivialized, patronized, limited, powerless. If I didn't want to accept this definition, how *was* I to speak of myself?

After internal argument, I found a rationalization which made me comfortable with the label. Calling myself an old woman was the radical way out of my dilemma. At sixty-eight, it may be presumptuous of me to assume a label which is descriptive of women in their nineties, but I have noticed that many of them avoid the term. Like other words which feminists are reclaiming by proud usage, I take to myself the word everyone seems to fear. My *real* circumstances will not suffer more than they have already. Nobody but radical women will stand there beside me, honest and angry about the distortions which surround the time of life all women dread. I will walk through the door-of-no-return and, from the other side, name the politics of age instead of waltzing around pretending I am just an "older" woman. The lies of age passing will not save me from the stigma of age. In fact, the invention and practice of most feminine wiles and deceits have kept women in harness, laboring to be someone who fits in, who pleases, who is chosen, who earns (and therefore deserves) love. I have grown sick of the harness.

Among my friends, lesbians like myself, the line between "older" and "old" is fuzzy, indistinct, avoided. Having found my personal path of resistance to the degrading dance of age passing, I discovered a burning need to share my insights with others. Isolation is part of the punishment of age. With high hopes, I set out to gather together a group of women committed to the discussion of ageism.

It was not easy to find women willing to focus on this subject. Most movement women see the problem as peripheral to "real" political issues. Ageism often is not even politically acknowledged, much less analyzed or confronted. Sadly, very few women recognize that ageism is the name of their emerging experience. Fewer still are able to separate ageist experience from the subtle changes in their expectations and the responses to them due to their aging. After many discouraging conversations with women who I mistakenly assumed would be interested, seven of us finally agreed to do consciousness raising together. As women who had always been involved in movements for social change, all of us realized that ageism was not part of the political agendas that engrossed our energies. Women's control of our bodies, racism, and anti-Semitism, rape, and battering — all are issues important to our political lives, but these are treated as if they had no special impact on mid-life and old women.

Some of us were friends of long standing; others were new to each other. We had no pretensions that we were a representative cross-section of mid-life women. Although most of us were white, able, middle class, middle aged and lesbian, there were differences. One woman was Black; two, Jewish; two, disabled; one, fat; one, heterosexual; one, old. Two had never had children; five were mothers of grown children. All were college-educated; our economic resources ranged from fair to marginal.

From my point of view, the age difference was too large. I was the only one of the group over the edge (no longer able to pass for middle aged), visually and by years.

The others were from five to twenty years younger than I. I was the only one who didn't identify as "older." But even for me, the other differences between us seemed more obvious, more dangerous.

From the beginning of our group meetings, the differences between our points of view muddled our communication. Although the others were eager to describe the ageism *they* experienced as mid-life women, only I seemed sensitive to the fact that all of us were involved in the dance of passing, with its relative advantages of one over the other. Our first get-together regressed quickly into a general gripe session. Although being in a group which talked about ageism was cathartic and empowering for me, being old in a group which consistently referred to old women as "they" was alienating. It is my hope that readers will listen carefully for the tension between the perspective of the *older* woman and the *old*. Hearing that differentiation may help them to become more finely tuned to their own age enslavement.

As I winced at a derogatory cliche, I began to recognize the magnitude of our group problem. All of us had accumulated enough years to have experienced some ageism. Each woman in that room was old in somebody's eyes. But unlike the others, I regularly got feedback from many people which told me that I was perceived as old. This was not true for the others. Looks are the primary criteria by which women are judged, by women and men alike. I looked my age. How were we going to be able to communicate with each other, when *old* meant so many things? The vocabulary of aging was mined with sometimes unintended negative innuendo.

Younger is not better, it is simply different. Embracing one's years means that old is good. Not better, just different from young. Years are an accumulation of experience which one does not deny, either in the changes they have made upon our bodies, the lines they have furrowed on our faces, or the quirks and strengths they have forged into our personalities. Typical uses of the words *young* and *old* ignore the disadvantages of youth whereas they emphasize the negative aspects of age. Here are some of the statements from the women in our group.

> When I have trouble getting up off the floor, for instance, I say, Oh, I'm getting old! It is a way of covering up other problems. It is easier to say than I can't get up because I'm disabled.

> •

> Or out of condition. The fact that I can't do it doesn't mean that another woman my age couldn't do it. In fact, when I say that, I am laying a trip on someone else.

> •

> It happens to me on an economic level. I find that younger women take it for granted that because I'm as old as I am, or because I have a steady job— for whatever reason—that I'll pay more than my share of the expenses.

> •

> If you are older, you are in charge.

> •

> If you're older, whatever you have belongs to whoever asks for it because *your mother never turns you down*.

I was talking about being old, the others were talking about being middle aged.

It is true that there is little understanding of the economics of age. When it becomes impossible to earn money because of age, one develops a generalized anxiety about money matters. How much will be enough? There are great differences between old women as a result of our work background, the career adjustments we have gone through, whether or not we have a pension or Social Security. Sensitivity to these anxieties should be part of the awareness of all women, not just old women.

Among the differences which divided the group was our relationship to employment. For women still engaged in the work world—no matter how problematically—the psychological impact of forced dependency, economic insecurity, and the denied productivity of old women was a distant problem. When a woman is part of the category *old*, she is presumed to be retired, that is, not working. Manual labor is not associated with old women; neither is remunerative employment. But no matter what old women do or don't do, they are seen as non-productive. Yet all over the world old women do much of the undesirable or unpaid labor designated in the culture as female work—agricultural work, child care, household maintenance, cooking. When younger women escape this work into the cash economy of factory or office jobs, it is largely old women who inherit the work which the younger woman can no longer perform. If women are the mules of the world, the grandmother is the mule's mule. And I do not mean just taking care of the grandchildren. The streets of the Soviet Union are swept by old women. In a socialist country old women are paid the lowest wages within the system for the hard, cold labor of cleaning the streets with twig brooms.

Employment was not the only subject in which our emphasis or priorities differed. We described to the group our particular experiences in the erosion of youth privilege. Youth privilege, like male privilege or heterosexual privilege, is made up of all those reactions and expectations which we were taught to take for granted throughout our twenties, thirties, and into our forties. It is a privilege of youth to anticipate that others will not expect them to share responsibilities, that others will grant them respect for differences, that a certain level of attention will be paid. Mid-life women correctly identify the erosion of these powers as age-related. But their solution is to develop further strategies for trying to remain "deserving" of that privilege. Women mill around in this trap trying to avoid thinking about getting old.

In the group, I struggled to give examples of my own confusion. "Recently I went to the woman's bookstore," I said, "where I found there were two whole shelves of different books in the category *Age*. I was pleased until I discovered that they were how-to books about 'getting old graciously.' 'Be positive! be content!' say these books written by young or middle-aged geronotologists, 'even though you are getting older?' But what about the societal constructs that make getting older hard? Take me. I will soon be seventy. I have become invisible. I am seen as asexual although that is not how I feel. I am condescended to and socially segregated, as if I had a disease that might be catching. And to top it off, I might find myself suddenly poorer. We are inundated by responses we cannot explain. To ourselves, we aren't all that different from what we were in our mid-life years. It is not physiological aging or psychological aging that is troubling me. I am experiencing societal aging— ageism. A generalized image is being projected upon me which does not correspond with my self-image. I must continually internalize this feedback or adjust to it in order to retain my sanity at all. It is disorienting and very hard not to lose confidence and blame myself. But this is not named for me in all these how-to books on age."

Young and mid-life women tend to see ageism as a continuing oppression of women throughout their lives. The point of view which I tried to voice sprang from my experience, which revealed abrupt changes in the degree or intensity of stigma when I could no longer pass as middle aged. I was uncomfortable with the absence of differentiation between the kind of ageism I remember experiencing as a teen-ager and what I am experiencing in my sixties.

I felt confused. I did not know how to integrate these concepts into my present circumstances. Was the pain over the ageism I experience intensified by the fact that my youth privilege had been augmented by the privileges of being white, able, thin, blond, tall, middle class? And how did all this relate to age passing, for many women try—and some even succeed by using repeated plastic surgery—to remain forever middle aged? For instance, the small, thin old woman—especially one who plays the cute social role—does not receive the same direct hostility that big motherly women do. Was the pain of ageism relative also, or was there a pall which settled over all old women (the year varying for different women) whether or not they had been pretty or middle class?

I began to recognize that no one in the group ever said to me, "Maybe you are experiencing more ageism because you are older than we are." As movement women have discovered, imaginary hierarchies of oppression can be very divisive. It was evident and disturbing to me that my investment in the issue of ageism was much greater than the others. When I challenged them directly, there was some acknowledgment of this difference. For instance, I said: "There are different responses based on different ages, even in this group. Let me give an example from another situation. We held a meeting for women over forty. I was feeling the need of exploring things that were peculiar to my sixties, so I asked for one session in which we divided ourselves by decades. This was unbelievably threatening to the forty year olds, who felt excluded. They felt that they had a right to hear what the older women had to say. I kept saying, 'Look, I am entering a time in which I have no models. I am exploring being a radical lesbian feminist in my sixties, instead of a door mat grandmother. I am trying to be here for myself, instead of for everyone else. I feel as if the perspective of the forty year old has always permeated everything. I don't even know what a sixty-year old perspective is.' "

Another time, I told them this story: "When the collective I worked with was meeting once a week to work on our differences, the youngest women acknowledged after a lot of very painful probing of their inner feelings, that some part of their minds were blocked when trying to think about their own aging. They said things like, 'Oh, I'm not going to get old,' or 'I'll be dead by then,' or 'I'll commit suicide before I get old,' or 'My life just isn't going to last that long.' I wouldn't let them get away with such an attitude. But while they were mulling over the irrationality of their position, I sat there thinking, 'Wow! They believe that they would rather commit suicide than to be like *me*!' We carry around a shield which protects us from identifying with women much older than ourselves, and hence, of seeing them at all.

Every decade is looking at the women ten or twenty years older as being substantively different. We are all doing it.

One of the first things we talked about was that we don't have enough models, since so many women around us are good patriarchal women who serve others — the cookie-baking grandmothers — so how do we know how we want to be? Throughout the first half of women's lives we cultivate a blank, an internalized non-person, a vacuum. Women are so afraid of age that we erase any image of our own future while we are still young.

I can remember when I was about thirteen, watching my mother and her sisters partying, and saying, very indignantly, "Why don't they act their age?" I am their age now and I party the same way. Who is to say what I am supposed to act like when I'm this age? *I never thought about being this age.*

•

I can remember having fantasies of things I wanted to do or be in my twenties, my thirties, my forties, and even my fifties. But now I have trouble fantasizing exciting new sexual encounters or imagining meeting Ms. Right whom I want to spend the rest of my life with or projecting adventures I want to have or believing that there are windmills worth tilting.

•

My fantasy life is twenty-three years old. I feel trapped. I stay here because I don't know where I am going or even where I want to go. I can't visualize what I will be doing when I am eighty years old. It's just not there. Knowing, as I do, that my future is shaped by whatever my image of it is, I've got a *real* problem.

•

Some terribly negative images have been substituted for my fantasies. My mother has been sick for about a year in a nursing home. I have been taking care of her and her affairs. The strength of my identification with what is happening to her is absolutely terrifying. When I forget or lose things, it is like *her* mind going. When I am not steady on my feet, it is *her*, not me. My fantasy of the future is to be in that nursing home. I want some of my old fantasies back!

•

Then the fantasies and the role models *are* tied together!

Because we were talking about fantasies, we were merging real issues of aging with ageist diseases of the imagination which we inflict upon ourselves. One of the things that women do when talking about these issues is to blur the distinction between aging and ageism. Aging is a real process which takes place differently in each individual. Ageism on the other hand is a constriction which rearranges power relationships, just like any other kind of discrimination or prejudice. When one ages, one may gain or lose. With ageism, one is shaped into something that is *always* less than what one really is.

There is the ageist cliche that all older women are mothers in disguise. Thus, when we exhibit leadership, competence, or political skills, we become psychological threats to other women.

•

When a younger woman feels inadequate or insecure around an woman older than herself, that is not necessarily a measure of fault in the older woman.

•

Yet older women are seen as a burden to the patriarchy, never a threat! One of the reasons that older women are invisible is that men define female purpose as reproductive or for sex. So what are older women *for*? Old women are always reminiscing about the days when they had a little power as mothers or wives. Memories do not constitute a threat to anyone.

•

But older women who have resisted on the basis of both their past and their present oppression could be a threat. There *is* a potential which older feminists are beginning to discover.

Our group discussions of death raised many issues of

ageism for me. Death is an extremely important subject which our culture has mystified, professionalized, sensationalized — and at the same time, made taboo. Everyone needs to make her or his peace with the meaning of death. However, the assumption that we mid-life or old women are preoccupied with death is ageist. The old should not be seen as standing with death at their elbow. Nor should the subject be age segregated. Repeatedly younger women make assumptions about my relationship to death. One woman said that she shared identity with me, because she had had many losses of people close to her in her life. She assumed that I had too. In reality, other than the death of my mother at the age of ninety-three, no one I've loved has died.

> I have been thinking about old women living together and helping each other to die.

> •

> I don't know that we can discuss age without discussing death.

> •

> One of the ideas which is important to me is the concept of having more control over the dying process.

> •

> Those who are dying are not supposed to admit that they are. We who watch them die are supposed to pretend that they aren't. This denial has a trickle down effect upon aging.

Here it was, that virulent stereotype — the age/death connection — unabashedly expounded in a group committed to exploring our own ageism! Apparently only old people die. Death does not hover near the cradle, the motorcycle, the toxic workplace, high bridges or battlefields. But around old women people are reminded that they have given their own possible mortality insufficient attention. Death is a forbidden subject with all but the old, who are expected to bear the burden of this social suppression. Since my own demise is as distant from my conscious mind as it was when I was twenty, I have come to recognize that it is my looks which evoke the age/death connection in others. Death has become a private buzz-word for me, warning me of the shoals of ageism before me.

I reminded the group that we were at the beginning of a world-wide demographic boom of old women. It is easy to predict that our society will soon be subject to all kinds of "new looks" at death and dying. I read a clipping from a futurist magazine suggesting that a demise pill be available to the elderly (but not the young, of course). The old are seen as half dead already. Old women, like everyone else, buy into the prevailing concepts surrounding both worth and death—we are as easy to brainwash as the next person.

Only one women, nearer than the others to sixty, expressed recognition of the oppression of the age/death connection. As time went on, I became acutely aware of the "voices not present"— the perspective of women in their seventies and eighties and nineties. When we talked about disability or fat phobia or poverty—all subjects that intersect with ageism—my understanding was expanded by the women in the group who could speak from their own experience. But we knew nothing of the special circumstances of age as it impacts on ethnicity which constructs its own problems and solutions. There are grim statistics which reveal the economic plight of old women—a demographic category with lower income than any other. There is a profession exclusively devoted to the study of age, gerontology. There are political organizations that promote the legislative and regulatory defense of the aged. Yet despite all this, we know next to nothing about what it is to be an old woman in this society.

How can old women begin to change this? First, we have to name our circumstances more clearly, identifying the root sources of our denigrated place in society. Feminist analysis and the concept of ageism are not used as tools by most old women. They tend to see problems as personal-interpersonal or physical or economic—instead of political. The time of life which should be a final ripening, a meaningful summation, a last chance for all the risks and pleasures of corporeal existence, is too often deadened by emotional isolation and self-doubt. As the average life-expectancy for women keeps creeping upward — almost into the eighties now — the quality of that life-to-be-expected keeps deteriorating.

The "natural alliance" which old women have a right to expect with mid-life women will not emerge until all women begin to recognize the pitfalls of age passing. Separating the perspective of the barely-passing older woman from my concerns as one-who-no-longer-is-able-to-pass has taken all my confidence and a great deal of hindsight. The mid-life woman feels increasing pressure — internal and external — about aging as well as the rejections of ageism. It is natural that she rushes to define the problem. In asserting her power over the insights of the old woman — the complaints, the accusations of ageism, the naming of the universal hatred of the Old Woman — she unconsciously silences the incipient radicalism of the only one who can tell her how bad it really is.

Old women need power. First, power over the circumstances and directions of our own lives and identity. Second, power as an influence upon the world we live in — the world we have served, in which we have such a large, unrecognized, vested interest. This is, of course, the rub. Patriarchal institutions are, without exception, designed to exclude the vision of old women. Most old women have little experience in leadership or influence. Mostly, old women know how to serve. The roles reserved and expected of women in old age — grandmothers, self-effacing volunteers to the projects and priorities designed by others, caretakers of old men — are custom-fit to our powerless status.

But there are ways that all women can begin to prepare the way for the empowerment of themselves in the future, when they are old. These changes can first be brought about in the women's community among lesbians and political women. The first step is for women to recognize that they have been programmed to hate old women and to deny them power. This brainwashing is so subtle that its eradication will take an effort equal to that which we have made and still must make upon sexism. Further, this brainwashing extends through our lives, making us fear the processes of our own bodies within time. These are attitudes and expectations which we can change if we decide to. Empowerment of women will come when we identify with women older than we are and not before.

Anti-Ageist Work

When we move to change our consciousness, we free ourselves of built-in disablers. When we share information with other women, we discover patterns in the problems we face. When we generalize the specifics of those problems into political actions, we devise women's shelters or abortion clinics or the legal/educational fight to reduce violence against women.

As long as the existing divisions between women encourage political impotence, we have to stumble along taking one step at a time. Perhaps the first step will be forming groups of young and middle aged women who wish to confront their own ageism. However, there is a danger in this similar to that encountered in male consciousness raising groups. Men used the opportunity not to explore their sexism but to exchange complaints about women — especially uppity women — and ultimately, to devise ways of resisting the momentum of women's liberation. (It was only when some men committed themselves to anti-sexist work and to female authority over the naming of sexism that some of them began to change.) Perhaps women in forming their own groups to combat ageism will fall into the same trap, complaining first about their mothers and then old women in general.

Another difficulty which I have witnessed in Ageism groups is the tendency of everyone in the group from eighteen to sixty to talk about the ageism which they experienced as teens (Adultism) or are experiencing as mid-life women. This is a valuable catharsis, but it will leave the prejudice against old women intact.

With these problems in mind, I have been devising a list of discussion topics for women who want to change their ageism. I have given copies to the few politicized old women I know and incorporated their reactions. I have tried them on a mixed age group of lesbians when I was living on women's land. These questions can be used in a group, or a woman can answer them to herself. This should not be used as a test to see how clean one is but to confront one's inner feelings:

1. "I can't help feeling that a mother is someone you *have*, not someone you *are*." What are your feelings about this statement?
2. An old woman often finds that other women expect her to see their needs as hers. *Her* priorities often become invisible. Can you describe situations from your life when you may have made this assumption?
3. Men go to war assuming they will not meet a bullet. Is this similar to your reaction to your own aging process?
4. When do you first remember encountering or feeling revulsion toward old women or the aging process?
5. When did you stop looking up to a woman older, more sophisticated, more wise than you?
6. When did you first sense that reaching a certain age meant a loss of power? What age? Over whom?
7. Describe times when you tried to pass for younger. To pass for older. What privileges were you seeking? In what ways do you anticipate trying to pass in the future?
8. When did you first notice that you treated older women differently than your contemporaries? How much older?
9. When you share confidences with a woman much older than yourself, what are your expectations of her?
10. Women face terrible pressure to hide their disabilities or their age. How do you participate in exerting these pressures?
11. Make a list of the terms or concepts which demean, trivialize or otherwise diminish women of age or mothers. Make another list of the negative stereotypes of old women which you remember from your childhood, TV, books.

12. Fill in the blanks: Older women always
    _____. When I am with older
    women I generally feel _____. I
    wouldn't want an old woman to _____.
    When with old women, I'm afraid I will
    _____.

13. Do you feel revulsion toward a woman's wrinkles, sagging muscles, stretch marks, sagging breasts, knobby joints, thin hair, facial hair, fat, poor hearing or sight? How about those possibilities or realities in yourself?

14. How do you feel about sex between two old women? Between an older woman and a younger woman? In the the latter example, who did you identify with? Whom do you imagine as the more empowered, the initiator, the possible exploiter? What age span is OK?

15. Old women find themselves "pedestalized" by younger women because of their accumulated experience. They also are stereotyped as dependent, decayed or incompetent. Discuss the whys and hows of these contradictory methods of distancing older women.

16. What did you learn from your mother or grandmothers about the aging process?

17. Do you speculate about the age of an older woman, but not about your contemporaries? Why?

18. How has ageism hurt you? How do you confront it in your daily life? Do you feel that you are actively anti-ageist, as opposed to "not being ageist?"

Afterword

There is the kind of change that happens, imperceptibly, like the sea fog that dims the sharp-edged greens and purples and reds of my sunlit garden, turning the vivid hues into fuzzy pastels even as I sit writing. How easy it is to forget the feel of color, the vibrancy. Adjustment to this new perception has encouraged me to deny the past intensity. That is the way I think of the changes which ageism has made in my life, between the years of fifty-eight and sixty-eight.

But inner change is not always imperceptible or unconscious. There are the changes which take exertion — the wrenching disruptions of attitudes, direction, values — changes like my creation of this garden by the sea, the gate, the flowers — even finding the time to write about the fog. All these have taken place in the same decade of my life. Because of changes like these I think of old age as a time of adventure. Aging is a familiar process to which I bring an ever-expanding Self, accumulated experience and a sense of urgency which dictates new priorities. It is not just the young who change as they get older.

It is fitting, then, that I end this book about the social malaise of ageism with a description of one such exertion — an event focused on ageism — which, in the words of a friend, "may have changed the rest of my life." Two hundred old lesbians from all over the United States and some foreign countries came together to "explore who we are, name our oppression, celebrate all that we represent, and make our presence a force in the women's movement." The call for the conference was specific and radical: *The First West Coast Conference By and For Old Lesbians*. Not older. Not elder. Just like it is — old. This uncompromising perspective characterized the whole event.

The women who organized the conference issued this statement:

> The 60 and older age limit was imposed because old Lesbians are especially sensitive to those younger Les-

bians and feminists who see themselves as committed to the old and tend to represent us, speak for us, and name us in ways that are self-serving, exploitative, and ageist. In some ways, 60 might seem a very arbitrary age. It was chosen because the degree of oppression is greater beyond mid-life, after 60, when most of us know what it is to be perceived as "old." In limiting attendance . . . we do not want to imply that being 60, 70, 80 or 90 are not distinct experiences, which we will be examining throughout the conference.

The organizing women said:

(As Lesbians) we have invented our own lives. We have expanded and liberated the meaning of being a woman. We are inventing our own aging. We want to share our discoveries . . . We want to analyze our experience of ageism, which has been so little defined, know how to name it and resist it. Society calls us "old" behind our backs while calling us "older" to our faces. We refuse the lie that it is shameful to be an old woman.

Since old lesbians are in many ways identical to other old women, most of us are still engaged in the great female preoccupation of age-passing. At many get togethers before the conference there was healthy controversy over the word "old." Would women voluntarily call themselves old? Some did not succeed and stayed at home. The age cutoff caused even more anxiety. Although each participant was allowed to sponsor the attendance of one younger lesbian, many in their late forties and fifties were enraged by what they perceived as their exclusion. The mid-life women who felt discriminated against were urged to organize their own conference. If they came to the conference, they were promised their own workshops in which they could look at their relationships with women older than themselves in the past and present. I do not know how many of these mid-life women learned from this to question their assumptions of experiential overlap, as well as the proprietary access they often imagine due them.

The conference opened with two presentations addressing the issue of ageism. One of the speakers, Barbara Macdonald, introduced important new theory on the psychological roots of the fear of age:

> We have become the old woman we dreaded to be, and find we like being who we are now. We live it with joy, and have come here to celebrate it.
>
> And yet there is still a dread that holds us back from taking charge of our lesbian power.
>
> What is it then that we dread? Is it not some unnamed fear of the future — something that keeps moving ahead of us but is never where we are? Doesn't the 60-year-old say, "I like being 60, but what will happen when I'm 70?" And doesn't the 70-year-old say, "Being 70 is exciting, but I don't know what I'll do when I'm 80?" And doesn't the 90-year-old enjoy 90 and worry about being 95, 96, or 97, and beyond?
>
> Isn't it true that we come to each of these plateaus of age and we look around for that thing we dreaded and say, "It isn't here yet — it must be something that comes later."
>
> Are we not dealing with a myth of old age — an accumulated deposit of everyone's fears of the uncertainty of life, which all of society has pushed ahead each year until it is compressed into the farthest end of our lives — and we, who are old, are expected to live out everyone's fear — not of old age — but everyone's fear of the uncertainty of life itself.[21]

After the opening session, the conference became highly participatory with a great variety of opportunities for women to exchange in both structured and unstructured situations. Needless to say, not all lesbians are — or even want to be — feminists, nor do all old lesbians want to be visible as lesbians. Many of the women who came to the conference did so primarily because they wanted to meet other old lesbians. However, all of us, political and apolitical, were expected to spend an hour and a half with age peers in a consciousness raising session. There we brought our own experience to the assigned questions: How does Ageism pervade our lives? How do we internalize it? What does it do to us?

There were two groups of women 71 and older; four, 65 to 70; six, 60 to 64; and two of younger women. In the group in their late sixties which I facilitated, there were several strong feminists. There were also women who denied experiencing any ageism in their lives; a woman who refused to tell her age; women who could not differentiate between aging and ageism; a woman who felt impelled to excuse and explain the ageist behavior that others described; women who wanted to talk about almost anything *but* ageism. As facilitator, it was my duty to nudge our discussion back to the unfamiliar ground of identifying the ageism which underlay so much else in our lives. It was not easy. I had been instructed to pose the question near the close of the session: "How does ageism benefit the patriarchy?" I reminded myself that we can only move in consciousness from where we *are*. Most women in their late sixties have not yet identified the structure of the society in which they live in terms of female subjugation. I wondered how many had an inkling how anti-ageist work could directly benefit their lives. Later in the day women came to me to tell me how much they had learned from that hour and a half.

The flavor of the total conference was so resolutely feminist, so determinedly anti-ageist that by the second day a bandwagon effect had begun to take place. Militant self-affirmation mixed with radical resistance to the stereotypical expectations of old women became normal behavior. Let me give an example. As we sat together in plenary session, a young lesbian, not a participant of the conference, took advantage of the open mike to appeal for our support and signatures on a petition to protect her rights to a job from which she said she had been unfairly fired. Militant old dykes came forward to protest this use of our precious time together, pointing out the ageism of her underlying assumption of the right to access to us. This small spontaneous happening sharpened our collective analytical wits. The awkwardness of that public moment when we, as a group, reversed our conditioning to be nice, to be polite and nurturing, to comply—that was cathartic.

When I had been asked by traveling members of the organizing committee what I wanted to see happen at the conference, I expressed real fear that the conference would be "professionalized." I needed an opportunity to exchange my experience with other old women, without the interpretations of so-called experts on age. While recognizing that younger lesbian gerontologists and therapists might well see "enabling" the conference as part of their professional duties I, for one, hoped that we could evade their influence. A critique of the ways that all the "helping" professionals (of any age) function in relation to those of us they perceive as their "clients" should be a part of the agenda of any conference by and for old women. And we, not they, should exercise the freedom of naming the issues important to us.

There is a basic contradiction between the interests of old women and the social workers, therapists and gerontologists who earn their livings working for agencies that study or serve the old. These agencies get their funds from politicians, foundations and individuals who must be convinced that the client groups are terribly needy—unable to take care of themselves, isolated, pitiful, helpless. In order to maintain a flow of money to pay their own salaries as well as to provide services, the professionals both objectify and stereotype us. All human beings go through periods in their lives when they are needy, including old women. And as we have all discovered, the sooner we escape that characterization of ourselves, either by other people or as a self-image, the faster we heal. In other words, although we may require the services—in part to offset the special problems which institutionalized sexism and homophobia have created in our lives—at the same time, we must conspire among ourselves to escape the image and the dependency which funding seems to demand and which professionalism seems to perpetuate.

It was apparent at the conference that my fear of the Geriatric Grab or the Therapy Throttle was shared by some of the women on the organizing committee. Both the morning and afternoon workshops were balanced between the political and the therapeutic approach. Women over sixty led workshops that ranged from "Ageism and the Myth of Ableism" to "Life as a Self-Fulfilling Process"; from "Old Jewish Lesbians: Anti-Semitism and Ageism" to "Sex and Sexuality from Sixty on."

What did we do for fun? The walls of the area where we met for plenary sessions and for entertainment were covered with photographs, paintings and objects of beauty made by old lesbians. Instead of Whistler's mother in a rocking chair, there were images of old women dancing together, old women naked, old women at work. We laughed and sighed over the love story of Eleanor Roosevelt and Lorena Hickok as portrayed by the brilliant over-sixty monologist, Pat Bond. There were songs and skits and a play, all of them performed by women at the conference speaking directly to our circumstances as old lesbians and old women. On Saturday night we danced until we could dance no more.

The momentum generated by all this energy and empowerment was not lost. Before we disbanded on Sunday afternoon, we had founded the International Association of Old Lesbians; pledged ourselves to another West Coast gathering in two years' time, as well as vigorous anti-ageist work between conferences. Women from the East made preliminary plans to sponsor an Old Lesbian conference there within a year. Volunteers came forward to work on compiling a dictionary of ageist terms and actions. Others wanted to create an anti-ageist consciousness-raising kit for use in small groups and for in-service training for Lesbian service providers, community organizers, and academia, including gerontology and women studies programs. The women under sixty formed the Anti-Ageist Lesbians, a support task force. The work of change for all old women—the wrenching disruptions and radical empowerment which we must accomplish for ourselves—has begun.

Sung Praises

Much has been lost as we have moved from an oral culture to a print culture; from being participants to being spectators; from being people whose cosmology was held with conviction and fervor to being docile consumers, the technological pawns without innocence or reverence. Sometimes music is a way to know this loss. The sound of women singing full-voiced in unison tells us of the changes we cannot remember. I do not mean the sound of singing along with Holly Near. I mean the assertion of the female folk choruses from the Balkans, or the sound of the Black *a cappella* group, "Sweet Honey in the Rock."

There must have been a time when women raised their voices together in passionate recital of a shared legend which praised a goddess figure. This was not a performance, for the ears of others. It was a ritual which had the power to evoke attention in energies beneficial to the participants. The doing of it was emotionally cleansing, an act of good health.

In addition to all the commercialized romance, women today have love songs of young women for young women; lullabies for children; blues which complain about our troubles; songs that protest our subordination. But there is one song which is mysteriously forbidden, forgotten, erased—the song in praise of the Old Woman. I am not the one to write this song, not because I cannot, but because I have lived too soon for it. It will spring from another consciousness which has only begun to re-emerge in the spiral of Time.

But I can imagine it. Can you? Picture on the screen behind your eyes a group of women singing as if with a single voice, full throated and joyously, a song in praise of an old woman, evoking the memory of her many years of bravery. Let them describe her courage, her strength in the face of danger, her craft and wisdom, the excitement of her ideas and the beauty of her old body and wrinkled face. Let them list the realness of her — her foibles, her style, her disabilities, her talents and skills. Let them tell of her losses as well as her triumphs. It is a love song to an old woman — making her a legend within her own time. Or it is a song to sing when she dies, to celebrate her transformation. It is a song which creates a magical unfilled space — which they used to call goddesshood — into which younger women may move and unfold. It is hard to say who needs it more, the old women or the young.

Notes

1. Barbara Macdonald and Cynthia Rich, *Look Me In the Eye: Old Women, Aging and Ageism* (San Francisco: Spinsters Ink, 1983).

2. May Sarton, *At Seventy: A Journal* (New York: Norton, 1984).

3. May Sarton, *As We Are Now* (New York: Norton, 1973).

4. Doris Lessing, *The Diaries of Jane Somers*, New York: Vintage, 1984).

5. Adrienne Rich, "Compulsory Heterosexuality and Lesbian Existence," *Signs*, vol. 5, no. 4. (Summer 1980).

6. Susan Sontag, "The Double Standard of Aging," *Saturday Review of the Society* (September, 1977).

7. Macdonald and Rich, *Look Me In the Eye*.

8. Ibid.

9. Ibid.

10. Ibid.

11. Rich, "Compulsory Heterosexuality and Lesbian Existence."

12. Lillian B. Rubin, *Women of a Certain Age, The Midlife Search for Self*, (New York: Harper & Row, 1979).

13. Colette Guillaumin, "Women and Theories About Society: The Effects on Theory of the Anger of the Oppressed" *Feminist Issues*, vol. 4, no. 1 (Spring 1984).

14. Macdonald and Rich, *Look Me In the Eye*.

15. Susan Hemmings, *A Wealth of Experience: The Lives of Older Women* (London: Pandora Press, 1985).

16. Barbara G. Walker, *The Crone: Women of Age, Wisdom, and Power* (San Francisco: Harper & Row, 1985).

17. Barbara G. Walker, *The Woman's Encyclopedia of Myths and Secrets* (San Francisco: Harper & Row, 1983).

18. Walker, *The Crone*.

19. Walker, *The Woman's Encyclopedia of Myths and Secrets*.

20. Ibid.

21. Barbara Macdonald, Speech, First West Coast Conference By and For Old Lesbians, California State University, Dominguez Hills, April, 1987.

The Crossing Press Feminist Series includes the following titles:

Abeng, A Novel by Michelle Cliff

Clenched Fists, Burning Crosses, A Novel by Chris South

Crystal Visions, Nin Meditations for Personal and Planetary Peace by Diane Mariechild

A Faith of One's Own: Explorations by Catholic Lesbians, edited by Barbara Zanotti

Feminist Spirituality and the Feminine Divine, An Annotated Bibliography by Anne Carson

Folly, A Novel by Maureen Brady

Hear The Silence: Stories by Women of Myth, Magic and Renewal, edited by Irene Zahava

Learning Our Way: Essays in Feminist Education, edited by Charlotte Bunch and Sandra Pollack

Lesbian Etiquette, Humorous Essays by Gail Sausser

Lesbian Images, Literary Commentary by Jane Rule

Magic Mommas, Trembling Sisters, Puritans & Perverts, Feminist Essays by Joanna Russ

Mother Wit: A Feminist Guide to Psychic Development By Diane Mariechild

Movement, A Novel by Valerie Miner

Natural Birth, Poetry by Toi Derricotte

Nice Jewish Girls: A Lesbian Anthology, edited by Evelyn Torton Beck

The Notebooks of Leni Clare and Other Short Stories by Sandy Boucher

The Politics of Reality: Essays in Feminist Theory by Marilyn Frye

The Question She Put to Herself, Stories by Maureen Brady

On Strike Against God, A Lesbian Love Story by Joanna Russ

The Queen of Wands, Poetry by Judy Grahn

Poems of Rita Mae Brown

Red Beans & Rice, Recipes for Lesbian Health and Wisdom by Bode Noonan

Sinking, Stealing, A Novel by Jan Clausen

Sister Outsider, Essays and Speeches by Audre Lorde

We Are Everywhere, Writings by and about Lesbian Parents, edited by Harriet Alpert

Winter's Edge, A Novel by Valerie Miner

Women Brave in the Face of Danger, Photographs of Latin and North American Women by Margaret Randall

The Work of A Common Woman, Poetry by Judy Grahn

Zami: A New Spelling of My Name, Biomythography by Audre Lorde